DANCING WITH A STAR

The Maxine Barrat Story

DANCING

WITH A STAR

The Maxine Barrat Story

Kristin Baggelaar

Midnight Marquee Press, Inc.
Baltimore, Maryland, USA

ISBN 13: 978-1-936168-27-9
Library of Congress Catalog Card Number 2012938171
Manufactured in the United States of America

First Printing by Midnight Marquee Press, Inc. December 2012

Dedicated to
Ginger Rogers,
American dance legend, inspiration
and dear friend of Maxine Barrat
and
my grandmother, Anna Kunigunde Kohl,
who made me feel like Ginger Rogers
when we danced to the "Tennessee Waltz"

Table of Contents

Acknowledgments

The backstory of *Dancing With a Star: The Maxine Barrat Story* is about the journey with many individuals who made it possible. Personal friend Sophia DelFavero devoted many hours of side-by-side research assistance—from visiting the Paley Center for Media to view the one extant episode of *And Everything Nice,* to scouring archived newspaper microfilm, New York Public Library document files, folders, photographs and 1930-32 John Robert Powers yearbooks—and in general made numerous trips to New York City sources very pleasurable. While Fia and I pounded the Manhattan pavement, my dear friend Albert J. Kopec worked behind the scenes, providing internet expertise and historical background—most especially in regard to early television—creating a Web site (www.themaxinebarratstory.kristinbaggelaar.com), critiquing rough drafts, copy-editing chapters, processing images and more. A childhood friend whose father worked for William Morris, Ruth Radam Quick, helped me try to piece together the years that Maxine was represented by this renowned talent agency.

Along the way I encountered the kindness of many professionals, notably June Reich, Archivist, Radio City Music Hall, who brought to light the accuracy of Loper and Barrat's 1940 performance at the venerable RCMH. For guiding me through Maxine's Florida years, I extend my appreciation to Archives Manager Dawn Hugh at History Miami Archives & Research Center; and to Bill Twomey for his historical insights of the Bronx. For bringing to life the sights and sounds of Maxine's first television show *And Everything Nice,* I thank the Paley Center and its staff. For making available their unique collection of photographs and a 1924 John Robert Powers yearbook, I am grateful to the staff of the New-York Historical Society. For helping me construct the events leading up to Maxine's career in television, I am grateful to David Weinstein.

The New York Public Library deserves special mention for its vast resources and the helpfulness of its staff in providing access to them; in particular, I would like to acknowledge the assistance provided by Phil Karg, Jerome Robbins, Dance Division and John Calhoun and others at the Billy Rose Theatre Division of the NYPL for the Performing Arts.

I salute the Fred Astaire family, especially Mr. Astaire's grandson Tyler McKenzie and longtime family friend Larry Billman for their dedication in honoring requests about films and dancers associated with Mr. Astaire, in general, and the Fred Astaire-Maxine Barrat connection, specifically; it was an honor to have made the acquaintance of such a fine family and I am very grateful for all their assistance.

Without the help of Maxine's assistant Nancy Shields, the inclusion of Maxine Barrat's entire personal collection of photographs and memorabilia might not have been possible—my heartfelt thanks for all your efforts, Nancy.

A grateful nod to Pat Carter Alders for sharing personal memories of her family.

Special thanks to Midnight Marquee author David Soren, who brought to my attention dance aficionado-editor-publisher Susan Svehla.

To Sue and Gary Svehla, we all are indebted to their integrity and devotion to the arts.

Foreword

For over a dozen years we've seen the magazine covers, talk show appearances, the heartbreaks, the through-the-roof ratings and the launching of careers. Well, fans of *Dancing With the Stars*—and all fans of the dance, the time has come to unveil both the underlying story of this ABC-TV juggernaut and a gold nugget of American dance history.

"What's behind this worldwide ballroom dance phenomenon?"

Cameras may take us into studios, observing rehearsals, dance-couple dialogues, fittings and finally *DWTS* contestants' performances, but the true story that sparked these contemporary miniature dramas actually took place many years ago. The *real*—and enduring—story is about an American dance legend named Maxine Barrat.

It all began with a World War I dance craze, propelled by Vernon and Irene Castle, America's high priest and priestess of dance. As Americans took to the dance floor between the wars, along came Maxine Barrat and Don Loper, "artistic heirs to the Castles" (*Look*, June 2, 1942). Their timing was perfect. It was the height of the Hollywood M-G-M musical extravaganza and the golden

Vernon and Irene Castle

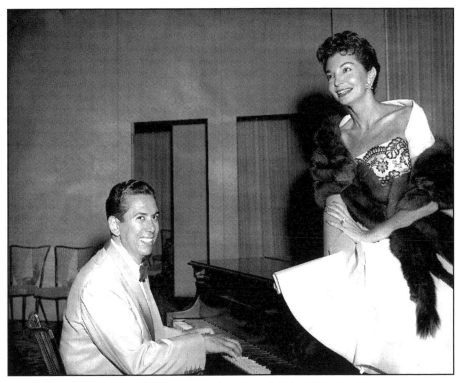

Pianist Carmen Cavallaro plays for a delighted Maxine Barrat.

age of supper clubs, when the elite and influential could gather to socialize over cocktails, dine on fine cuisine, dance to the strains of legendary bands and be entertained by all the top acts of the day. Loper & Barrat's big break came at the world-famous Copacabana nightclub, where they set foot onto the dance floor as a fledgling act and were fast-tracked into the annals of entertainment history.

Now this bold spirit, female trailblazer and true-to-life legend, Maxine Barrat, is unwittingly at the center of today's dance buzz. Behind the scenes she still turns heads as she did when her name was headline news years ago—a pop culture star of old made new again. She is at once the megastar *and* the professional dancer celebrated via *Dancing With the Stars* and *So You Think You Can Dance,* which features brilliant young dancers working their hearts out to make it as professionals in their field.

Her story is the stuff of dreams—riveting, exotic, passionate—from fracturing her back as a child in a dance recital fall that put her in a full body cast for almost half a year, to sneaking into Radio City Music Hall as a teenager to watch her idol Ginger Rogers on the silver screen; to dancing in the arms of Gene Kelly in her first Broadway show; to appearing in a second Broadway production costumed in yards and yards of flowing white silk in a winter gown and ermine-lined

Maxine visits with Ginger Rogers on her ranch.

hood, specially designed for her by renowned Vincente Minnelli, who was still working on Broadway and had not yet made a name for himself as a great film director.

A stint at the glamorous Copacabana catapulted Loper & Barrat to international stardom: ocean voyages to Rio and Europe; a special performance for the King of Denmark; and an M-G-M film contract to star with Kathryn Grayson, Mickey Rooney, Gene Kelly, Judy Garland, Eleanor Powell, Lucille Ball, Red Skelton, Lena Horne, Donna Reed and more, in what has been called "M-G-M at its Best," *Thousands Cheer.*

"Will you dance with me in my next film?" Fred Astaire asked Maxine, and she flew to Hollywood for a screen test with him. She reinvented herself as a nightclub singer, donated her time and talents to the war effort and continued her stellar career in the world of fashion. Then a phone call from a DuMont Television Network exec, "How would you like your own TV show?" and it was back to New York and a new career in the up-and-coming medium of television. Maxine's sensational life is interlaced with those of the stars she befriended, from Katharine Hepburn and Ginger Rogers, to those with whom she danced and romanced—from admiring South American *caballeros*, Hollywood moguls and stars, to a one-and-a-half-year affair with *Gone with the Wind* matinee idol Clark Gable.

Maxine Barrat is a performing arts legend who holds a vital key to the American dance story. She is the *real* star.

It's time to put Maxine Barrat back on the dance floor.

Introduction

I first came across the name Loper and Barrat in 2006 while doing research on the history of the Copacabana. It wasn't long before I realized that this team was not only one of the premier ballroom dance acts of the day but arguably the force that turned the then-struggling nightclub into a world-famous phenomenon.

Much to my delight, I discovered that Maxine Barrat was not only alive, well and living in Florida—but she was presenting a one-woman show and *still* modeling. Any trepidation in reaching out to an individual, who has earned a place in the pantheon of ballroom dance, was immediately dispelled by her warm, engaging and self-effacing phone presence—a strikingly down-to-earth demeanor for someone of her stature, I thought. This delightful lady responded to my request for some photos with a note and four pictures:

> Dear Kris,
> What a splendid idea, to do a story about the "Copa" AND Thank you for asking Don & me to be a part of it.
> The picture of us is one I think you will be pleased with.
> The picture in the lilac outfit is me now at 91 & still modeling in fashion shows.
> I also do a show called "Chocolate Bars to Caviar" in which I show pictures & tell stories about the Copa. The picture of me signing autographs—they have just seen "Chocolate Bars to Caviar," and loved it.
> I included the picture with Ginger Rogers because she came to see Don & me at the Copa. She invited us to her table after the show—that's how we met—she and I remained friends for over 30 years.
> Just "ring my chimes" if you need any more info.
> Great good luck.
> [signed] Maxine

I had an opportunity to meet this engaging former Copa superstar when she accepted my invitation to participate in a Copacabana book-signing reunion at New York City in October 2007. She was every bit as genuine in person as she had seemed over the phone. Utterly charming, full of life and fun—yet strikingly humble.

She invited me back to her hotel room to look through memorabilia that she had brought from her Bonita Springs home. Over dinner at Sardi's, where we sat at the same table once reserved for her and Don Loper at the height of their theater and nightclub career in New York, we discussed writing her life story.

Maxine today

Some time passed. My attitude toward her story slowly evolved from mere interest to fascination; I was hooked. I realized that hers was not only a wonderful story—about the mid-20th-century American dance scene, the golden age of nightclubs, the spectacular Broadway and over-the-top Hollywood musicals, early television and its expansion in Florida and more—but one that unveils a preeminent female American performing artist who has significantly impacted our cultural history.

But no trumpets blaring here, no need—Maxine's glorious story speaks for itself, from the heart—filled with humility, kindness and passion.

It is the real deal. It *is* Maxine Barrat.

PART I

THE STREETS OF NEW YORK

Chapter One
Audition Lessons in a Broadway Theater Balcony

Freezing, thought the men on the breadline. A bone-chilling dampness of a Manhattan holiday season. It was midday. The country was in the midst of the Great Depression and yet there was a steady murmur of automobiles, shuffling feet and the ubiquitous bustle in Times Square. Groups of men and women desperately seeking work gathered in front of employment agency offices. Some men stood in the streets, sullen and hollow-eyed, wondering how they were going to feed their families; others banged hopelessly on door after door of warehouses and businesses that had managed to survive the market crash. Still others ended up standing on street corners, selling apples for a nickel.

Out of work along with professional people, lawyers, doctors and engineers, were hundreds of theater people, actors, stagehands and ushers, whose jobs were cut as Broadway producers trimmed expenses amid unprecedented economic turmoil. With increasing difficulty producers such as Lee and J.J. Shubert, Sam Harris and Max Gordon continued to present a number of acclaimed musicals and more sophisticated revues, but the number of productions declined dramatically as the Depression deepened.

While the cost for even a one-dollar balcony seat was beyond the means of many citizens, the theatrical amusements of the Great White Way still parted the clouds of the Great Depression for those less financially scathed and held out hope of cultural opportunities in the future for those less fortunate. In the famous playhouses west of Broadway, the Broadhurst, Shubert, Morosco and Music Box, among them, theater people lucky enough to still have jobs were eager to sate audiences hungry to put their daily woes far away.

It was to these august side-street theaters off 44th Street that the legitimate shows had relocated when they were driven out of Times Square itself by motion pictures, a burgeoning medium that took a huge percentage of Broadway talent during these hard times. The heart of this venerable theater district was the famed Shubert Alley, which divides the block between Eighth Avenue and Broadway from 44th to 45th Street. It was here that actors and chorus girls and boys eagerly queued up when shows were being cast.

There was a creative energy, an inextinguishable vibrancy, in spite of the bleak climate of the 1931-1932 Broadway show season. Enthusiastic young men and women, high on hopes of theatrical glory, dashed excitedly along the city sidewalks, hurrying to casting calls or dress rehearsals, in and out of stage door entrances. Their thoughts were a world away from the desolation that lay just outside the magnificent Manhattan playhouse walls.

At the time there was one play in particular that captured the imagination of a very special teenaged girl, who waited eagerly for the November 29,

1932 opening night of Cole Porter's *Gay Divorce* at the Ethel Barrymore Theatre. Or maybe it was the buzz surrounding the show's leading actor that piqued her curiosity. A celebrated Hollywood hero of that era, debonair Fred Astaire, had been cast to perform for the first and only time on stage without his principal partner and sister Adele. It was a leading role that required singing and acting in addition to the fancy footwork for which he was famous. While gossip columnists opined about his ability to handle these challenges, the inquisitive teenager pondered, "what would it be like to dance with Fred Astaire?"

Fred Astaire and Claire Luce in *Gay Divorce*, 1932

The following year Fred Astaire would team up with Ginger Rogers, an idol of many young female dance hopefuls—and especially this one teenaged girl, who watched the famed dance duo again and again at Radio City Music Hall. But for now the girl's interest was held by Astaire only in the role of Guy in *Gay Divorce*.

Tryouts and rehearsals went on as usual for other popular shows of the day, *Dinner at Eight, Flying Colors, Music in the Air, Of Thee I Sing* and *The Dubarry*. Young women toting round hatboxes filled with dancing attire dashed to and fro, occasionally bumping into one another at theater side doors, laughing, apologetic and giddy with anticipation. Young men engaged in lively conversation, jostling one another on the steps or in the doorways, as eager to speak with one of the beautiful girls as to land a role in a show. Amid the constant stir it was difficult at times to tell who was coming and going at the stage doors. No one seemed to notice if anyone managed to sneak in or out. Nobody seemed to care.

One day, as a young female performer hurried to an audition, she was unaware that the same pretty teenaged girl who had dreamed of dancing with Fred Astaire was following close behind her. When the young female performer passed through the stage door, the teenaged girl darted in right behind her, unobserved.

Once inside the theater, the teenager quickly dropped back. She smiled reticently, pleased with herself for slipping by unnoticed. The bold plan that she had dreamed up had worked. She had managed to sneak into the theater for the auditions scheduled for that day.

She stood quietly at the side and took in her surroundings. The theater was dark except for a work light illuminating a small area directly over the stage and spilling into four or five rows of seats. Fixed within the beam of light was a single performer, poised and ready to audition. The teenager noticed other young women in rehearsal clothes standing to the side, waiting their turns.

Suddenly, she panicked, thinking, "If they ask me to audition, I'm in trouble! I better make myself scarce."

She retreated swiftly further into the backstage area to hide and plan her next move. Even though she was a naturally gifted dancer with many years of classical ballet training, she was naive about trying out for a part. She didn't have the faintest idea of how to audition. It was the missing rung in her climb toward a professional dance career.

She needed to find out.

Edging ever so stealthily, she made her way to a side door, passed through it and was back outside. She walked swiftly along the exterior of the building, found another door a few yards away and re-entered the theater at the main floor in front of the stage. Crouching down so no one would see her, she took in her surroundings and got her bearings. She dropped down onto her hands and knees and started to crawl slowly up the lushly carpeted aisle, from the front row of rich, maroon, velvet-upholstered seats all the way to the back of the pitch-black theater.

Cautiously she pushed open one of the double swinging doors leading from the rear of the orchestra section into a lobby that dazzled with rich woodwork and ornate chandeliers. The lobby was deserted. She dashed across to the grand staircase leading to the first mezzanine on the opposite side. Taking the steps two at a time, she climbed two flights of stairs and reached the second floor of the theater. She traversed the dark, wide hallway, gently swung open one of the double doors and entered the rear of the balcony section. Groping her way in the darkness down to the front row, heart pounding, she sank deeply into one of the plush cushioned seats.

With her gaze intent on the proceedings below, she sat silently, mesmerized, her forearms crossed over the balcony railing. All afternoon she watched one performer after another come out on stage to audition.

From her secluded perch in a Broadway theater balcony, a passionately determined 17-year-old named Maxine Boura observed, listened and learned what to do, what to wear and how to act for an audition.

Now she was ready.

Chapter Two
Discovering Ballet

"My parents would peek out at me dancing on the porch and say, 'There she goes again'!" Maxine vividly remembers. Even as a child Maxine's strong, innate will to dance would spring to life at the least provocation:

> They'd be playing music and I would start to dance. There wasn't enough room in the house, so I started dancing on the porch. It was like a stage for me.
> I remember the house—and the porch, which went all the way around. I used to dance all the way around the house.

The two-and-a-half story, wood-framed home purchased post-World War I by her railroad ticket-agent father, Hippolyte Boura, was situated on a double lot on the north side of East 235th Street. It stood in one of the scattered residential neighborhoods of the northeastern part of the Bronx known as Wakefield. Along the front of the Boura property at number 670 was a darkly colored wood picket fence, which echoed the pattern of similarly hued columns and balusters of the wrap-around porch, where Maxine danced with such joy and abandon.

Most of the frame houses and cottages on 235th Street were privately owned, painted various colors, fenced in and gated. There was an absence of driveways and an abundance of open curb space, as automobiles did not become a common family possession until after World War II. Tall deciduous trees between the sidewalk and curb provided shade as well as a country ambiance to the tranquil neighborhood. The modest, well-kept homes were the realizations of dreams for many of the middle-class residents, who took pride in their tidy lawns, flowerbeds and neat gravel walkways. Their leisure hours often were spent enjoying wooden platform swings, hammocks and front-porch rocking chairs that were popular neighborhood fixtures at the time.

Maxine's childhood home (courtesy of NYC Municipal Archives)

The Boura home between Carpenter Avenue and White Plains Road, the area's main shopping area, was conveniently located and within close proximity to many neighborhood amenities. The nearest public elementary school, P.S. 16, was within easy walking distance at East 240th Street and Carpenter Avenue. The Wakefield Casino, popular among local families for its clambakes and picnics—and among the men for thirst-quenching cold lagers—was located at East 239th Street and White Plains Road. The nearest police station was the 27th Precinct (now the 47th Precinct), located south of East 230th Street, next door to the 63rd Engine Company firehouse.

While Maxine was enjoying typical childhood pastimes in her own little world of Wakefield, free-spirited girls known as flappers were dancing the Charleston, frequenting speakeasies and nightclubs, shredding Victorian restraint and redefining modern womanhood. She and her family attended movies at the Wakefield Theatre, which opened in 1928 at East 234th Street and White Plains Road, less than two blocks from the Boura home. The Laconia Theatre at East 224th Street and White Plains Road opened in 1926, and two years later the Burke Theatre opened on nearby Burke Avenue. With the release in October 1927 of the first feature-length movie presented as a sound picture, *The Jazz Singer*, talking pictures or "talkies" became all the rage. Motion picture houses flourished.

Flappers, who embodied the modern spirit and new dance styles of the Jazz Age, now fueled a general enthusiasm for dancing that had begun at the turn of the century. Society's fashionable, elaborate cotillion had waned in favor of the waltz and two-step, which in turn yielded to more intimate modern steps like the turkey trot, the tango and the foxtrot. In 1926, a new frenzy began with "I'd Rather Charleston, " written for and introduced by the brother-sister dance team of Fred and Adele Astaire in the London production of *Lady, Be Good!* Everyone was dancing the Charleston.

The stage was set for Maxine to take ballroom dancing to new heights in just a few years.

Once called "the beautiful Bronx" by area residents, it was an exciting place to live during the boom years following World War I. Newly extended subway lines now made the Bronx

The Jazz Singer **opening at Warners Theatre**

Dancing with a Star

easily accessible from Manhattan. Maxine's home was only two blocks from the 233rd Street station of the IRT (Interborough Rapid Transit Company) subway line that still exists today and runs from the Bronx to Brooklyn. As it was an overhead—or elevated train—in this section of the Bronx, it was commonly called the "el" and often referred to by its last stop, the 241st Street and White Plains Road line:

> My father worked for a railroad company that ran a line up to Westchester. This is how we happened to move to this area. They [her parents] felt that the country was a better place to bring up a child. My dad kept saying: "It's so beautiful up there. It will be a nice place for the girls to stretch their legs and play tennis."

Prior to moving to the Bronx, the Bouras had resided in a large shingled single-family home at 274 West 131st Street in Manhattan. Its colonnaded front porch wrapped partially around one side, serving as the impetuous very young Maxine's en plein air dance stage. The larger front porch at their new home in the Bronx provided a bigger expanse for Maxine to express herself through dance.

From its 19th-century rural beginnings, the Bronx grew rapidly into a thriving suburban community. Millions of hard-working, culturally diverse, middle-class men and women left the crowded streets of New York City to make a better life for themselves and their children in the fresh air, wooded acres and tree-lined avenues of the Bronx, once part of Westchester County. *The Daily*

Argus newspaper, published in the Westchester city of Mount Vernon just to the north, was subscribed to by many Wakefield residents as it covered the news of their nearby section of the Bronx.

The Wakefield populace was once largely German, mostly truck farmers, and later shopkeepers, as well as employees in the area's thriving piano industry. After the turn of the century the ethnic population began to shift as many of the German families moved away and the Irish, then Italians, moved in. These cultural changes were reflected in some of the local religious institutions. St. John's Methodist-Episcopal Church on Richardson Avenue became a Lutheran Church and circa 1917 became St. Anthony's Roman Catholic Church, with services conducted in Italian. The cultural base expanded further during the unprecedented growth and prosperity of the Roaring Twenties, when an influx of newly transplanted Manhattan tenement and apartment dwellers brought new cultures and traditions to the northernmost reaches of New York City, now linked and easily accessible by IRT and IND (Independent Subway System) subway lines. Families settled side-by-side into villages called neighborhoods, each with its own dominant ethnic identity representing every face of the borough's ever-expanding population of Germans and Irish, Italians, Russian and Polish Jews, blacks and others.

Born on February 28, 1915, Maxine inherited from her lovely North Carolina-born mother, Monica (neé Kennan), a warm, gentle spirit and open-minded religious values:

> My mother had a poor background; my dad, too; but she had the most beautiful outlook on life. Even though she was brought up in a convent and my dad was an altar boy—so naturally, they were very good Catholics—my mother did something unusual in the Catholic religion. She did not baptize my sister or me. She believed that we should explore life and it's meaning for ourselves and make our own decisions. She knew there was more than she had been taught and she wanted us to find out for ourselves. She felt that other religions had a lot to offer—she would never change hers, she would die a Catholic—but she wanted us to have a choice. If I had a Presbyterian friend, I went with her to a Presbyterian church; and if I had a Jewish friend, I went to the synagogue on Saturday. I acquired a respect for all religions.

Her mother, a practical nurse, also instilled in Maxine an appreciation for music and artistic expression. While blessed with a beautiful soprano voice, Monica Boura never sang professionally, but Maxine fondly recalls her mother's singing for her friends at church and parties, bedtime serenades of Irish folk tunes and Broadway melodies and sunrise reveilles:

> She would start to sing and we knew it was time to get up. She'd wake us up with her beautiful natural voice. What a way to wake up! It was wonderful. Some operas, some popular music—her voice could carry and handle both.
>
> My mother loved opera. She had recordings that she could listen to and she'd go to the opera once in a while. They didn't have the kind of money that they could go whenever they pleased, so it was a treat for them, when they would go.

Interestingly, one of the most highly regarded opera singers of the 19th century once had lived only a quarter of a mile from the Boura residence. At 4718 Matilda Avenue between 241st and 242nd Streets was the family home of famed coloratura soprano Adelina Patti for whom "Sweet Adeline" was written. Today Adelina Patti (1843-1919) is probably best known as the great-grand aunt of Broadway actress, singer—and namesake—Patti Lupone.

From both her parents Maxine acquired a love of theater:

Adelina Patti

> They took me to theater from the time I can remember, and that's where, I guess, I opened my eyes to what was happening around me.
>
> Sometimes I would go to the ballet by myself, when I was around the age of 11, 12. I couldn't afford an orchestra seat, so I would buy a seat up in the boondocks, then sneak down, wait until the show started, see an empty seat and take it so I could be up front to watch. I never got caught!
>
> I *loved* theater, and I just wanted to see the ballet dancers *so much*.
>
> At that point, I thought, "I have to have a ballet career."

Mirrors, mirrors and more mirrors. The local dance studio walls were covered with mirrors. A young Maxine, trying to perfect a classical ballet position while poised on barre in front of one of the mirrors, frequently stopped momentarily to smile slightly at another girl who was watching, admiring her. Maxine's innate talent was evident from the very beginning. Other children in her ballet class often tried to emulate the beautiful lines, arcs and balance in her moves:

> I didn't know that it was a gift, really. You don't know that at that age. I just loved to dance. I was dancing all over the place. At the slightest provocation, I was making all sorts of ballet gestures. I guess I was just a natural.

Initially Maxine's parents believed that Maxine's desire to dance to music was nothing more than a childhood whim. It seemed innocent enough—and conventional especially for little girls—to let their daughter take lessons, so the Bouras readily agreed:

> My parents thought it was just a childhood thing. They would say, "She has talent. She can dance and move well and she is having fun." So that was great…up until they knew that I was getting serious. That was a different story.

Unlike so many of the little girls who took ballet and then moved on to sports, musical instruments or boyfriends, Maxine was one of the few whose love of ballet only grew over time. A passion for dance soon consumed all her time and energy. As she became more and more involved with her dance classwork, engaging her heart and soul in her assiduous study of ballet and perfection of technique, her mother fretted about her passion for dancing. She urged Maxine to broaden her horizons:

> My mother said, "Come on. You have to learn more than just dancing. You must learn to play the piano, like your sister."
> My sister, Marie, played the piano *beautifully*. She was a concert pianist at 15. We had a piano at home and we both took lessons, but I wasn't very good at it. It wasn't my forte at all, but she played like a dream.

While ballet lessons had been a part of her life from the time she can remember, Maxine's recollections of her earliest experiences are vague:

> There was a small studio. I think it was a private family, someone in the neighborhood who gave ballet lessons. It seemed to be a very small room in a private home. It was a small ballet group, only four or five children.

In this small private setting, the foundations for her training were laid. As a very young child, Maxine learned the importance of a good, slow warm-up as a safe start to ballet practice. She and the other youngsters most likely would have giggled in amusement as they stretched, practiced good posture and worked to increase the strength and flexibility of their small, growing muscles. They did exercises, like sitting on the floor with necks and back straight, stomachs in, feet together and pushing their knees down to learn "frogs" to help them turn their legs out.

After the family's move to Wakefield, Maxine continued her ballet lessons in a more structured, formal atmosphere:

> By then I was in a studio with good trainers in regular dance classes. I took ballet, tap and some modern as well. I was thin—all arms and legs. I had the body of a dancer.

Maxine excelled. Her strong, lean legs, arching neck, lengthy taut arms, exquisite hands and long fingers and finely modeled torso were ideal for a dancer. Her body moved with a power, grace and fluidity that made even the most difficult techniques seem easy. She perfected her body alignment and balance and became adept at coordinating the visual with the physical elements of dance, training her eye and her body. With practice she developed an ability to bring together the correct look with the feeling within her body. By recognizing this association she was able to master a sense of correct placement—proper posture with lines projecting from the body in proper alignment.

Her intermediate and advanced classes always began with long, slow handrail or barre exercises, arduous and monotonous, but a fundamental necessity to avoid injury. Warming up before dancing is always one of the hardest rules for exuberant young students to learn; but it is a discipline that is the foundation to meet the ballet's physical challenges and help to facilitate longevity as a dancer.

Outfitted in leotards, tights and ballet shoes, hair neatly pulled away from the face and neck, secured with hairpins or pinned up in braids or a bun, Maxine

Maxine with her best friend Beatrice

and the other girls would take their places at the barre and begin warming up. As they worked on placement, they patiently and thoroughly prepared their bodies for the hard work to follow. Legs and feet turned out sideways, she and the others would practice the five positions from which the circular and linear combinations and all the movements in ballet are derived. Simple steps, harder steps, combinations of which became sequences—or *enchaînements*—would be woven together to make increasingly complex and interesting dances.

The highlight of each dance school season was the annual, end-of-season recital. Students of all ages worked tirelessly for weeks and weeks, preparing to go on stage and put on a show in front of an audience. Routines and complicated steps that can take months or even years to master were practiced over and over again. Fourteen-year-old Maxine Boura, the school's star pupil, was prepared to give the most stunning performance of her young lifetime.

What happened instead almost ended her dance career forever:

> We were doing a sort of dance-play. We were on this beautiful stage with an Oriental setting. There was a stairway that went up quite high in the middle of it, and a high priest was at the top of this flight of stairs.
>
> I was supposed to run up this stairway and talk to the high priest because I had been a naughty girl. He was supposed to forgive me, but he didn't like my story, so he stabbed me. I would turn and twirl and fall. A young man would be there to catch me and we would do our dance routine.
>
> During rehearsals, he caught me very nicely. But one time, I ran up those steps, the high priest stabbed me, and I twirled— but nobody was there. I fell and hurt my back severely.
>
> An ambulance came and took me to the hospital, and they put me in a cast from my shoulders to my hips.

Maxine had suffered a serious hairline fracture of her spine. The body cast limited all movement, and she was restricted to lying on her back on a flat board—not even a bed—at all times for months.

After a few months passed by, Maxine asked, "Well, is it happening? Is it healing?"

She was assured that her back was healing; she had to be patient. Then she overheard a conversation between her mother and the doctor that spurred her into action:

> I overheard the doctor talking to my mother. I guess I wasn't supposed to hear, but I did.
>
> "We took x-rays, and they're not very good," he said. "Now don't be surprised if she can't walk again. She *may* be able to

Maxine with her first partner Leonardo—she made the dress she is wearing from her mother's curtains.

walk, but she'll never dance. That was a pretty bad fall." He was very emphatic.

I froze. Not dance? What does he mean? I have to dance! It's my life. It's everything in this world I ever wanted to do.

From that moment on, I decided, I better get to work here. So I started to work my feet, making small circles, trying to use my leg muscles. I put weights on my feet and moved them up and down so they wouldn't get weak. I would move my legs and if it hurt my back, I'd stop. As the days went by, I started to use them more.

Then a physical therapist said, "Maxine, you seem to be doing very well."

"I feel great," I said. "Why can't they take off the cast?"

"Don't be impatient because you'll end up on your back again," he told me. "You have to let it heal properly."

In the meantime, he gave me a rod to hold in my hand so I could do exercises with my arms. So then I was doing exercises with my feet and my arms and trying to keep my legs and arms strong. This helped enormously.

One day, after about four months, I thought, I've had enough of this. I'm going to get up. I tried to get up, and I fell right back down. I couldn't get up.

Finally they took the cast off about a month later. To my surprise, my legs *could* carry me and my back was pretty good. It was painful, naturally, because it was still healing. Gradually, *gradually*, I started to move, and walk, and then do little dance steps. And the first thing you know, I was dancing. I was so grateful to be able to move again. And I went on with my dancing.

Maxine's urge to be a professional dancer grew stronger: "At some point, I said to my mother and dad that I thought I wanted to be a professional dancer. My father went into orbit. 'No daughter of mine is going to go into theater,' he told me."

Hippolyte Boura was adamant. In those days decent folk frowned upon the idea of a nice girl going into theater. The Bouras were dead set against a dance career for their daughter. It was unacceptable. They would not tolerate it. They cut off the allowance money that Maxine had been using to pay for dance school.

But Maxine was determined to continue her lessons. She had to find another way to pursue her passion.

Chapter Three
The Kindly Ushers at Radio City Music Hall

The IRT subway rumbled along the steel rails, carrying passengers from the far reaches of the North Bronx into Manhattan. A teenaged Maxine Boura watched as blue-and-white station signs above the splintery platform boards flashed by the subway car windows, mesmerizing her. On opposite sides of the car's interior, long rows of seats were arranged with their backs under the windows. Passengers sat, faces glazed, staring blankly at one another or out at the diverse scenery flashing past the dirty windows. Maxine shifted her position on the tattered cane seat in the overcrowded, confined space, but the surroundings didn't distract her from a reverie, pondering her destination and the purpose of her trip into New York. On this day, as on so many others, the young dance hopeful had her heart set on seeing her idol Ginger Rogers dance with Fred Astaire on the giant screen at Radio City Music Hall.

By now Maxine was riding the White Plains Road and 241st Street subway line frequently on Saturdays when school was not in session. It was an easy walk to the 233rd Street station just a few blocks from her house. This train line suited her needs nicely, taking her down the west side of Manhattan to West 59th Street, where Eighth Avenue and Broadway cross at Columbus Circle, before veering slightly east to 50th Street. This was her favorite stop—and one that Maxine knew well.

New York City, 1933

A MUSICAL EXTRAVAGANZA
STAGED IN THE CLOUDS!

FLYING DOWN TO RIO

with
DOLORES
DEL RIO
GENE RAYMOND   RAUL ROULIEN
GINGER ROGERS   FRED ASTAIRE
MUSIC BY VINCENT YOUMANS
DIRECTED BY THORNTON FREELAND
MERIAN C. COOPER-Executive Production

As the subway sped over the tracks, passing farms and empty lots, single-family frame homes, store signs, apartments, factories and coal yards, Maxine daydreamed about her future, her destiny to be a professional dancer. Despite the landscape's bleak signs of a ravaged economy, closed playgrounds, boarded up businesses, banks and libraries, Maxine was filled with optimism. Large single doors, three to a side, opened and closed as passengers boarded at stops along the way. Some of the riders held onto the pole in the center of the car when there were no longer any vacant seats. Overhead, wide four-bladed fans, which were activated in summer to move hot, sultry air trapped in the enclosed space, were idle on this bitterly cold day. Only the squealing of the metal wheels and the *click-click click-click* of the car passing over the joints between adjoining rails reminded Maxine that she was on a journey, not a stage.

While the financial meltdown of the Great Depression took a severe psychological toll on many Americans, the effervescence, wit, energy, movement and style of mass entertainment buoyed a beleaguered morale and stimulated hope for the future. Zany comedies, glorious musical extravaganzas and even machine-gun-rat-a-tat-gangster films propelled audiences toward a brighter side. Big Band swing music and the magical dancing of Fred Astaire and Ginger Rogers took us there, too.

As the subway screeched to a halt at the 50th Street platform, Maxine sprang to her feet and pressed with the rest of the passengers toward the opening doors. She made a dash for the stairs that would take her to street level and headed in the direction of Sixth Avenue. In another year or so she would wander over to Broadway or walk west toward Eighth Avenue, seeking out young women who might lead her to dance studios; but for now, Maxine was intent on seeing the new RKO comedy-romance musical, *Flying Down to Rio,* at Radio City. Everyone was talking about the music, the stunning costumes, the splendid scenes of Rio, the amazing finale with a bunch of smiling girls strapped to airplanes—and above all—the dancing. Even though Fred Astaire was cast as second male lead and Ginger Rogers had only a small role, the movie was the milestone that gave us the debut pairing of the most popular dance team in film history.

Ginger Rogers was one of Radio City Music Hall's biggest box-office draws, with 23 films playing a total of 55 weeks in her long and successful career. In 1982, she was honored at a special dinner held on the RCMH stage for having had more films open there than any other female star. Fred Astaire was second only to Cary Grant as box-office champ, with 16 films playing a total of 60 weeks:

> On Saturday, when I didn't have class, I would go there, especially if Ginger Rogers and Fred Astaire were there [in a film]. I would be there at 10 o'clock in the morning, when Radio City Music Hall opened. I would go in and sit there *all day* and watch them. Ginger Rogers was my inspiration.
> I would sit there and watch them and think, "I can do that."
> All the ushers got to know me so well they'd let me go out and have lunch and let me back in without paying a second time. I'd sit there until six o'clock at night when I knew I better get myself home in time for dinner.
> That's how I got my inspiration, watching them.

Depression-era Saturdays commonly were reserved for going to the movies, and typically thousands of people flocked to Radio City Music Hall—Showplace of the Nation. It was a magical place, where even the poor and middle-class could enjoy a feature film and a spectacular themed stage show. There was a symphony orchestra, world-class ballet, choral ensembles and celebrated singers performing arias and cantatas, all for an affordable price. Radio City was perhaps

Flying Down to Rio is remembered mainly for the daring and exciting dance numbers in the film.

the grandest of the old motion picture palaces, or presentation houses, and the largest movie theater at the time of its opening on December 27, 1932. It was a phenomenon. There was always a crush and constant flow of people entering and exiting the cavernous 5,933-seat auditorium from the early morning to the late, late show. The breathtaking great stage, which resembled a setting sun, and the slowly changing rainbow of colored lights during the presentation delighted audiences of all ages.

I wasn't the brightest student. I tried, but I was too interested in dancing.

I remember a funny story. At the end of the year we were taking final exams. In the middle of a major exam I thought of a wonderful step combination. I stopped everything—and under the desk, I started to tap, tap, tap. I started working out this pattern, tap, tap, tap. I thought, "Oh, this would be a beautiful move!" I was working out the steps. "Oh, it would be great if I did this, instead of that. This would go fine!"

The teacher came over and said, "Young lady, *what are* you doing?"

At a complete loss as to how to explain my behavior, I sat silently. The teacher said, "You may leave the classroom." I was thrown out of class!

Somehow I managed to get out of high school.

That nothing seemed beyond Maxine's reach in the performing arts, however, was not lost on her Wakefield dance studio instructors. Her parents were enraged when she told them that she wanted to pursue a career in dance; but, as dead set as her parents were against her wish to become a professional dancer, Maxine was equally determined to pursue her dream:

At some point I had said to my mother and dad I thought I'd like to be a professional dancer. They were against it. They didn't want me to spend any more money going to a dance studio for lessons. They cut off my dance money, but they didn't cut off my movie money; I was allowed to go to the movies. Instead of going to the movies, I went to the dance studio where I had been studying, and I told them what had happened.

I asked, "Can I teach a class?" That was the only way that I could think of to continue with my dance lessons. They said, "Of course you can." So they let me teach a ballet class. I was able to help the little ones. I was able to give a good class. Then they gave me a class. So I earned my lessons.

While in high school, one of her instructors asked Maxine to dance with him at the end-of-season recital:

He asked me to be his dance partner. Of course, I was thrilled to death. By this time the idea of being a professional dancer was developing in my head. I didn't *really* realize it so much then, but as I think back now, I can see where I was beginning to put down my roots as a professional dancer.

Out of all the students in the class, I was the one he picked. He was so wonderful. He saw a spark in me, he told me later.

Maxine couldn't tell her parents that she would be a star performer in the recital, but she wanted them to be there:

When it came time for me to do this recital with my instructor, I told my mother and dad that I was working backstage and invited them to come. I was afraid to tell them I was in it. I thought well either they're going to throw me out of the house, which my dad could have done very easily—he was that adamant about it—or they're going to accept the fact that I have to dance. So they came and sat in the audience and out I come, dancing with my instructor. They were not prepared for it.

You never saw anybody as nervous as I was before I put my foot out on that stage. But you know, it's a strange thing about professionals—and obviously I was a little bit of a professional even then—to this day, I'm nervous as all get out; but, the minute my foot is out on that stage I'm as calm as can be. Something happens. You know you have a job to do, and you do it. You're dying one minute and you're calm as can be the next. Something happens within you. It's a great desire to do the best you know how. It's a tremendous burning desire. You want it to be right. You want it to be great. You want to use what talents God has given you, what the soul is meant to share—the joy. It's a deep feeling.

Maxine and her instructor-partner's performance brought down the house:

The audience is always very generous with youngsters, of course, but we were good. We were really good together. I could feel his tempo and the emotion that we were supposed to have in it, the joy and the beauty. It was all there.

I was a natural. I had a God-given gift.

As he [the instructor] told my mother and dad later, "She's a natural. This should be her life."

I had told him beforehand what was happening. He was well aware of the situation. I had said to him earlier, "Would you please talk to my mother and daddy? I don't know how they are going to take it."

So he came out with me afterwards and he talked to my mother and dad. He had met my mother before, but he hadn't met my dad.

"Wasn't she magnificent?" he asked, trying to build me up at that point.

"Yes," my dad said, "but where is it going to lead?"

"She has a God-given talent," my instructor answered. "Let it lead where it will."

"Daddy, we've got to let her go," my mother said. "She's a natural. We've got to understand that."

I had a little trouble convincing Dad, however, but he realized—he didn't want to—you know, that kind of reluctant feeling. He wanted to say, well, certainly you can do something else.

So I said, "Well, if I don't make it in the theater, and I may not, because I know it's a tough profession, I'll study to be a teacher." I'd been reading avidly about all these other people who had been in the theater. Every time I'd get a magazine, a theater magazine of any kind, I'd read all this stuff because I wanted to know more about their lifestyle and how they got into the business. I was trying to find my way. Needless to say, we didn't know anybody in the theater.

He calmed down a bit that night, but he tried to talk me out of it for a couple of months. After that night he kept saying, "You're a beautiful dancer, yes, I know, but that's only one career. You should have a back-up career just in case it doesn't work out."

So he was trying to prepare me, and rightfully so, because even with talent, you never know. I've seen so much talent that never got a break. I was blessed. I *did* get a break.

I agreed to study to be a teacher. I would have been a lousy teacher because I wouldn't have had the patience. He wanted me to be the principal of a school—that was his big ambition for me. I thought, "Ooh, that's the last thing I wanted to do!" But he's being good about it, so I'll try to satisfy him and tell him I'll study to be a teacher. I was still in high school and I had my regular education to get through, so I didn't have to worry about ever pursuing teaching.

By then it was too late. He had come around and accepted that I was going to be a dancer.

Chapter Four
A John Robert Powers Model

I don't know if I would have tried modeling if it hadn't been for my sister Marie. I don't think so—probably not. She kept encouraging me. She kept saying, "With your natural graceful ability you should be a model."

Marie Boura's lovely face and figure adorned the pages of the leading women's magazines of the day, *Vogue, Harper's Bazaar, Ladies' Home Journal.* It was the post-World War I period of revolutionary social change and more relaxed fashion styles. Marie Boura was one of the faces of this new look. Her exuberance, confidence and enthusiasm ignited Maxine's imagination. With her success as a high-fashion model, Marie became a motivating force behind Maxine's own lifelong modeling career:

Marie in Paris, 1926

Marie was my inspiration. I'd see her do all these wonderful things—all the modeling—and think, "How marvelous!" She'd tell me about it and show me all the pictures. I loved it! It looked so glamorous. That's where I got my desire.

She was a top model in New York. She'd walk into one of these offices that hire models and they'd *find* something for her.

She was very beautiful. She was 12 years older than me. She had different coloring completely, very light, light skin, gorgeous pitch-black hair and *huge* blue eyes. She was a knockout, a *real* knockout. A natural beauty. I was not by far. I was the brown wren, so to speak. I was all arms and legs. I had a typical dancer's body, which I didn't realize—I didn't appreciate—at the time. I just hated it because she was so soft—a nice rounded, beautiful figure—and here I was, long arms, long legs. We were two different types.

As 20-year-old Marie related stories to her younger sister about the photo shoots, designers and fabulous clothes she modeled, Maxine was held spellbound. Marie's word sketches of her friends and other models, like Joan Crawford, intrigued Maxine. "She and Joan Crawford were modeling at the same time. They were good friends."

My sister adopted the name Billie. She didn't like the name "Marie" so she adopted the name "Billie." We called her Aunt Billie.

There was some sort of conversation between my sister and Joan Crawford. Billie [Joan Crawford] said, "Why don't you adopt my name if you don't like yours so much?" My sister said, "Oh, I love the name. You don't mind if I use it, too?" They were such good friends. My sister admired her so much, her talents and everything; she was so inspired by her, so she adopted her name.

Her sister Marie's world of the 1920s held Maxine in wide-eyed wonder. It was an optimistic and prosperous time, when fashion was evolving and entering the modern era and reflecting women's newly found freedoms and independence (the 19th Amendment of the U.S. Constitution giving women the right to vote became law on August 26, 1920). Traditional dressmaking by seamstresses was in decline, brought about by the increasing popularity of women's attractive and less expensive ready-to-wear clothing produced in factories. Now the average woman was able to afford an array of stylish hats, gloves, shoes, dresses, skirts, blouses and suits right off the rack. Corsets gave way to revealingly clinging sheath dresses, shorter to show more leg and embellished with sequins, fringe and colorful, reflective beads that underscored a loosening of social morals and a new energy. More popular were shorter skirts and dresses with relaxed pleats, gathers or slits and looser, dropped waists and wider hips, which allowed more movement. Other new looks—rolled stockings, flamboyant hat styles and trousers—all marked the advent of women's sportswear. The carefree and comfortable styles reflected a relaxing of social constraints and a changing role and larger presence of women in the workforce. Advertising was the linchpin in the promotion of awareness, acceptance and advantages of ready-mades, and models played a key part in revolutionizing the way women dressed.

Maxine gazed longingly at the pictures of her strikingly beautiful big sister posing in the latest fashions of the day. The clothing sported labels of some of the big houses—H.I. Gross, Sidney J. Stern, Harry Angelo and Maginnis & Thomas Importers—or the fashionable New York City department stores B. Altman and Lord and Taylor. As eight-year-old Maxine looked at Marie's 8x10 photographs and portfolio of magazine print ads and listened to the fantastic, alluring stories behind them, she continued to dream, waiting for her turn on the world stage.

Eager to follow in her sister's footsteps, Maxine began her journey into the world of fashion modeling in the early 1930s. At age 17, she marched boldly into the formidable Park Avenue offices of the John Robert Powers modeling agency, where Marie Boura had made a name for herself. "I had a lot of nerve,

A teenaged Maxine in one of her earliest professional photo shoots

thinking I could follow *that*—my sister's fabulous reputation—she was so successful and *so* gorgeous."

John Robert Powers modeling and talent academy, established in 1923 by former actor John Robert Powers, had set an industry standard and had gained a reputation for its clout. The prestigious title of "Powers Girl," the natural, poised American girl—synonymous with beauty, refined elegance and glamour—was much sought after and considered a feather in the cap of a young woman in Marie and Maxine's day. While the Powers clientele was predominantly female, some men were part of, and benefited from, the agency's "be yourself" philosophy, *"Be Natural."* Some Powers models became Hollywood's leading men and ladies of the mid-20th century, including Frederick March, Tyrone Power, Joan Blondell and Barbara Stanwyck. Many became successful on stage and

Maxine models swimwear in 1937

television or made their mark as great socialite beauties.

Maxine was hired. "I was young, but I had a sophisticated look." During high school, after class, on weekends and after graduation, Maxine was part of a modeling powerhouse that steered the public to products manufactured by industry giants in all fields.

She quickly rose to the status of one of John Robert Powers' top-flight models. Although she was not tall enough to be a high-fashion model, Maxine found her own niche. The more modest bathing suit styles of the 1920s had given way to backlessness, smaller overskirts and more décolletage, largely brought about by a vogue for sunbathing in the early 1930s. Maxine excelled at modeling the new bathing suit styles—and fishnet stockings—with a shapely pair of legs that would rival those of 1940s icon Betty Grable. She also became a foremost model for one of the best-known household brands in the country, Hanes.

Maxine's print ads promoted major brand names, such as Elizabeth Arden, Coca-Cola and many others:

> The print ads were photographed at various studios where there would be huge background drops that could be changed in a wink into all sorts of colors and designs. It was set up that way—easily changed. And, of course, a lot of the photography was done live during a fashion show.

In later years, Maxine became a model for Revlon. Maxine was going out on her first modeling interviews when the company was founded in 1932. Initially Revlon offered only one product, a new type of nail enamel. Within a few years, the company was selling a variety of nail enamel shades in drug and

A head shot of a young Maxine

department stores. Later a line of lipstick, cosmetics, manicure and pedicure and hair products was introduced, making Revlon one of the largest, most popularly priced brands in its industry. Originally black-and-white artist renderings, Revlon magazine ads became full-color photographic advertisements in major magazines and stores across the country by the mid-1940s, and Maxine was front and center in their advertising campaign: "I was blessed with beautiful hands and nails, so I did a lot of hand work for hand creams, nail polish and cuticle enhancement."

Maxine lotion ad, 1937

In the years before World War II, women rarely went out without a whimsical hat or a millinery headpiece called a fascinator. Some millinery designers believed that one of the functions of hats was to lead a way out of economic recession by their exuberance. The brimless millinery staple—the cloche (shaped like an inverted bell) hat—and the expensive, elegant wide-brimmed hats of the 1920s gave way to closer-fitting, asymmetrical, sideways-tilted styles. Cloches of the 1930s were updated with an up-turned brim, and other styles—button plate, snood, pillbox, French beret—came into fashion, reflecting the mood and financial constraints of the Depression years. New designs framed the face rather than hiding it. Slouched felt-brimmed hats worn Greta Garbo-style were paired with the new sportier clothing, while shallower styles were used to accessorize dressier attire. Also popularized by Garbo was the "Eugenie," a little skull-fitting ostrich feather-trimmed hat with a rolled brim worn tipped over the right eye. Designed by Adrian, best known for his costumes in *The Wizard of Oz* and other M-G-M films of the 1920s-'30s, it recalled a style worn decades earlier by Empress Eugénie, wife of Napoleon III. The Eugenie became wildly popular after Greta Garbo wore it in the 1930 film *Romance,* and it dominated the millinery scene throughout the decade, it was later even worn by Princess Diana in 1980. Maxine's perfect model head size made her a natural for modeling hats of all kinds:

> *Hats*! I loved modeling hats. That was another big part of my work. I modeled hats like crazy! And I *loved* it—it was fun. I had a perfect model's head size, 21-and-a-half inches, which is not very common—it's usually 22, 23.

Maxine's dual careers as fashion model and dancer would seam perfectly together a few years later, when she would wear outfits, hats and gloves designed exclusively for her by dance partner Don Loper. "I had *even more* hats and gloves!

"Everything came together."

Chapter Five
In Pursuit of Girls Toting Round Hat Boxes

Dark clouds over the United States Capitol mirrored the country's despair as Franklin D. Roosevelt was sworn in for his first term as President of the United States on March 4, 1933. It was the depths of the Great Depression. F.D.R.'s customary charm and wit were all but absent as he delivered a solemn inaugural address, declaring to a demoralized citizenry, "...the only thing we have to fear is fear itself." It was a message of assurance for a nation beaten down by economic crisis—failed banks, factory closings, joblessness, cityscapes dotted with families scavenging municipal dumps for food and some dwelling in tarpaper shelters. In spite of the hardships of these dark days, each morning dawned with a semblance of normalcy. Manhattan's smart hotels continued to host delightful events, like fashion shows, where beautiful young models showcased the latest styles and hairdos and cheerfully lifted the spirits of audiences eager for a look toward a brighter tomorrow.

On May 20th and 21st, 1933, Maxine starred in her first major theatrical production. She was cast in the lead female role of Patricia Harrington in *The Patsy,* a 1925 Broadway hit and 1928 silent film (starring Marion Davies as Patricia Harrington). The three-act drawing room comedy by Barry Conners was a Little Theatre of Schiff Center production of the Thalian Guild of the Jacob H. Schiff Center. The venue was part of a prominent Jewish cultural center and synagogue in the Fordham section of the Bronx near the Boura's Wakefield home. While Maxine would become more famous as a dancer on stage, she would also garner numerous credits for legitimate acting roles.

Maxine's personal life, however, momentarily threatened to derail her professional goals. She had become involved with a young man named Joe Levine, with whom she heedlessly tied the knot. Maxine quickly realized that the marriage was a mistake, and it was later annulled:

> Joe and I were teenagers. I met him in school. I was married
> to him for only a few months. That's when I said to him,
> "There's no point in my being married. I will never be here.
> I will be traveling over the world." I knew in my heart that I
> was going to be a dancer.

Meanwhile, Maxine's modeling career was on the rise. She had begun what would be a record-breaking, eight-decade career as a fashion model, yet she felt restless, unfulfilled. Maxine always knew that she was destined to dance professionally and her passion never wavered. She had overcome preliminary hurdles—a serious spinal fracture, her parent's vehement disapproval of a

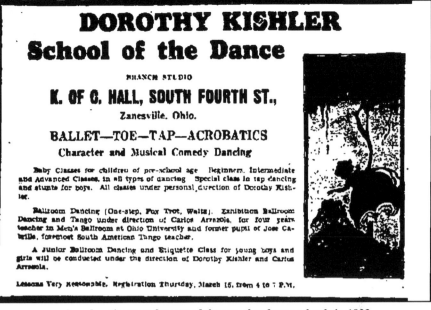

An advertisement for one of the popular dance schools in 1933

professional dance career, as well as figuring out how to audition—but now
she faced another challenge. It was the most daunting of her early career and
required the utmost perseverance and faith as it was largely beyond her control.
For the first time she came close to giving up.

Her artistic drive and determination alone were not enough to achieve
success nor was merely the mastery of her body-instrument. She felt that she
had gone as far as she could go on her own. Maxine was at a crossroads.

It was then, as it would be at other times in her life, that Maxine reached
deeply into the essence of her being and found the will to go on. Even though
she always had stayed true to her dream, it was not until her late adolescence
that she embraced what would become a lifelong attitude: Life has more in
store if you don't give up.

Maxine's thoughts gravitated back to a seed planted the very first time she
saw Fred Astaire and Ginger Rogers move as a perfectly synchronized unit on
the dance floor. She was sure that this phenomenal duo held the clue to her own
success. It was becoming more and more clear to her what she needed—what
was missing—to move ahead.

What she needed was an ideal partnership, one like her idol Ginger Rogers
had with Fred Astaire. Only with a superlative ballroom dance partner, who
shared her passion and complemented her every move, would she be able to
break through onto the world stage. The problem was where to find a perfect
male dance partner. It was the beginning of an odyssey that would take Maxine
from one New York City dance studio to another many times over.

Want to Dance Well? Watch Fishies; They Have Rhythm

By H. ALLEN SMITH
United Press Staff Correspondent

NEW YORK, (UP)—People who are unable to dance and would like to learn should go to some aquarium and watch the fish swim, according to Arthur Murray, one of the world's foremost authorities on ballroom dancing.

"A person," said Murray, "can get an idea about rhythm by watching the fish. They've got it. And after you've watched them swimming, it would be a good idea to go out and ride a horse. That also provides you with a sense of rhythm. In fact, you can observe almost any animal and find an innate rhythm worth studying. Take a jackrabbit for instance."

Murray's studio might aptly be described as a "dance factory." They give lessons to more than 1,000 persons daily, and employ 160 instructors.

In one large studio today 50 new teachers were undergoing training because Murray believes repeal of the 18th amendment will stimulate interest in dancing, and more people will be wanting to learn how to do it.

"We have people that come here," he said, "and pay as much as $1,000 to learn how to fox trot or waltz. Some of them keep on coming long after they have learned. We have some who have been coming twice a week for the last seven years and paying for it. Murray doesn't believe there will be any drastic innovations in ballroom dancing soon.

More Conservative

"People adapt their dancing habits," he said, "to the tempo of the times. You remember what the war brought—all that jiggling and jumping. Ballroom dancing is getting more conservative all the time. The waltz is coming back into favor. The atmosphere of the old days is bringing it back. Perhaps Mae West has something to do with it. I can remember when people danced like stark mad fools. But it's much different now."

Murray said that he, personally, has taught 20,000 men and women to dance. In all these, he had but two failures.

"They just couldn't do it," he said. "They were mentally abnormal. Everyone has an inborn sense of rhythm and it's only a question of getting it under control. We had a man come here once. a famous singer from the Metropolitan Opera company. He couldn't dance at all. I had him beat time with his finger and he was perfect. I had him nod his head to the music. He didn't miss. But he couldn't control his feet.

Dancing Instinctive

"But dancing is instinctive. You will find children who never heard of dancing, doing it when they hear music. Everybody has to do some dancing in his lifetime. If it isn't done when you're young it'll get you in your old age. Look out here."

He indicated the reception room where a dozen or more customers were awaiting their turns. Half of them were past 60, and one man was nearer 80.

"We have many of them in their 70s and 80s," Murray explained. "They come in and say they want to learn to dance, and that they'll pay liberally if the job can be done. And they do it."

American attitudes were changing. Heretofore the darling of European society, ballet was setting down more permanent roots in America. The growing interest in ballet was reflected in the increase in visiting foreign dancers, notably the Russian ballerina Anna Pavlova, the Ballet Russes and Vaslav Nijinsky.

On January 2, 1934, George Balanchine opened the doors of the School of American Ballet at 637 Madison Avenue, New York City, with an enrollment of 32 pupils. The founding of a major ballet school and company was another signpost of our country's recognition of the dance art form. Ballanchine's company initially had a limited New York season and a brief touring schedule. By the 1950s, there were several different ballet companies boasting more well-attended New York engagements as well as tours to major U.S. cities. Modern dance was developing in America and Germany. American innovators like Martha Graham, Doris Humphrey, Mary Wigman, Ruth St. Denis and Ted Shawn were reshaping dance forms and receiving widespread acclaim. The general public was embracing concert dancing, which once belonged to a select urban audience. Economic stress and competition from abroad were making American dancers more creative and adaptable, and they began to reach beyond the highbrow concert stage to find a new market in "legitimate" and musical theatrical productions. Successful groundwork laid in revues by Genee and Lopokova, Fokine, Albertina Rasch, Doris Humphrey and Charles Weidman (*Americana*, 1933) paved the way to the opening of other profitable markets and receptive audiences in hotel cabarets and nightclubs. Dance was coming of age in America.

During the 1930s, Americans seemed as keen to take to the dance floor as to sit and watch a performance. Dancing became a popular pastime—a form of recreation—for the public at large. Ballroom dancing was hot. On July 2, 1934, six months after the founding of the School of American Ballet, Arthur Murray leased 30,000 square feet divided into private dance studios on seven floors at 7 East 43rd Street in the heart of Times Square. As the demand increased more and more studios opened. At any given time all the modern ballroom dances—the waltz, foxtrot, rumba, samba, tango and swing, which was taking the country by storm—were learned, practiced and performed on the thousands and thousands of square feet of dance studio floors throughout the city. Dance studios for those who have a talent for or love of dancing, amateur and professional alike, have been thriving ever since, especially in recent years.

While the cost to attend presentations of theater dance forms was prohibitive during the Depression, the reasonable price for a movie ticket made it possible to bring dance to people who might never have had the opportunity to enjoy it otherwise. It might have been beyond the means of many Americans to see Fred Astaire in the 1932-33 Broadway production of *Gay Divorce,* for example, but it was affordable when it came to the screen in 1934 as *The Gay Divorcee*, starring Astaire and Rogers.

The advent of television not only further leveled the economic playing field, it brought dance into our very own living rooms. Today the high Nielsen ratings—and commercial success—of reality TV dance shows like *Dancing With the Stars*, are a testament to the resurgence of ballroom dancing made popular in the 1930s and '40s.

Growing acclaim brought students from around the globe to New York. Some of the premier names in the world of dance taught at the more prominent studios, many of which also boasted well-known graduates. By 1936, while Maxine was searching intensely for a partner, there was a formidable array of offerings in the midtown area alone. Former Metropolitan Opera ballet master, choreographer and respected teacher Luigi Albertieri opened the Albertieri Studio in 1915. There he presented classical ballet lessons by his protégé Salvatore and Spanish dancing by Paco Cansino, uncle to actress-dancer Rita Hayworth and instructor-mentor of Emmy-Grammy-Oscar-Tony awards winner Rita Moreno. Tap dancing specialist Jack Stone had a studio at the corner of 53rd Street and Broadway; next door, at 1697 Broadway, Adolph Blome at the Waiman Studios provided special instruction for dance teams in developing grace, poise and showmanship; Miss Alma, a few doors down at 1690 Broadway, was a ballroom dancing specialist. Two blocks away at Broadway and 51st Street was Fred LeQuorne, a foremost instructor and coach to some of finest dancers of the day: Veloz and Yolanda, Gomez and Winona, Florence and Alvarez, June Knight, Harriet Hoctor and others. Fred LeQuorne's impressive staff of specialists offered unsurpassed instruction in waltz, tango, rumba, bolero, modernistic, musical comedy, tap and ballroom. Paul Mathis, formerly with avant-garde dance pioneer Ruth St. Denis and Ted Shawn, advertised a style

George Balanchine teaches a class at the School of American Ballet in 1936.

of training called the Denishawn technique; his studio offered "practice classes for professionals, evening classes for business girls, special classes for men and Saturday children's classes." These and other studios, regardless of prestige, scope or size, provided nurturing environments with instruction and coaching for students of all ages in all forms of the dance. For many of the dancers a studio became a second home.

While some studios were well publicized or had window signs easily spotted by gazing up at second, third or fourth floors of buildings along Broadway and Eighth Avenue, other studios that were tucked away or not designated with a sign were hard to find. Maxine realized that she would need someone to lead her to the more hidden locations. She was determined to search out as many dance studios as possible in her quest for a dance partner. She had a plan:

> After I graduated from high school, I continued with my modeling, but every time I didn't have a job or was inbetween jobs, I tried to find a partner.
> But I didn't know where to go to find one.
> I finally learned to go over to Broadway. I would stand there with my little round hatbox with my dancing clothes in it and watch for girls to go by with a similar box. I knew they were dancers.
> I'd follow them.

Dancing with a Star

Sometimes I would wind up in a subway station because they were going home. Sometimes I ended up backstage because they were going to an audition. And sometimes I ended up at a dance studio—and that's how I found out where the dance studios were.

I'd follow these girls, end up at a studio and stay around there for a while. I'd talk to people. Or I'd go in and watch a class and get a little familiar with the people, what they had to offer.

The scenario was much the same time and again. Maxine would see a young woman carrying a dancer's telltale small round tote and fall into step behind her, keeping a few paces back. By dodging in and out on congested sidewalks Maxine could keep her distance from, but her eye on, the tote-carrying girl who might lead her to a new dance studio. She hoped that she would get lucky and not only get a fresh lead, another contact for a potential dance partner—maybe even find *the perfect match.*

A typical outing might go like this: Maxine would spot a girl dancer in Times Square and follow her as she crossed over the median at 42nd Street, headed west, rounded the corner at Eighth Avenue and walked several more yards, stopping in front of a plain, unmarked door. Opening the door, the girl, her guide, would go into into a poorly lit, tiny vestibule with a row of wall-mounted metal mailboxes at the bottom of a worn, narrow wooden stairway, and start her ascent. Immediately Maxine would dart inside and start up the stairs, closing the distance between her and the young dancer. While there might be several doors off the second-floor landing, only one was of interest to Maxine—the one marked with gold-and-black decorative lettering affixed to the frosted inside surface of its paned window designating it as a dance studio. On the heels of the young girl, who unknowingly had brought her there, Maxine would enter the newly discovered dance studio. There she would have another chance to fulfill her dream.

Inside would be the usual dance and rehearsal studio accouterments: floor-length mirrors mounted around wallpapered or painted walls, an expansive hardwood floor space, velvety drapes separating dressing spaces in the studios, benches and barres. Dancers clad in flimsy rehearsal costumes, short ruffled skirts and other practice clothes would infuse the atmosphere with kinetic energy, tension, exuberance and an air of freedom. Some dancers might be poised at the sidelines, striking a typical ballet stance, a stretching of the neck, heads immobile or upraised with the arms; others moved about with a gait, an eloquence, peculiar to dancers. Still some might be warming up their agile bodies at the rows of barres or practicing movements learned during recent classwork. One or two high-spirited dancers might be peeling off pirouettes, practicing skips, leaps or sustained extensions, spinning, gesturing sensually.

Workshops or classes might be in session conducted by talented instructors of various backgrounds and teaching styles, and a pupil might be taking a lesson in an acrobatic or interpretive dance in one of the rear compartments as a Victrola played a 78-rpm recording of a popular tune like the "Winter Waltz." Maxine reminisces:

> Most of the studios were walk-ups, second-story, and very simple, nothing fancy, just plain studios with lots of mirrors and lots of barres.
> There were the usual workout classes. Good teachers and a lot of ambitious young ladies and gents who wanted to make a career of dancing. They thought they were good dancers and wanted to further their careers, looking for a partner.
> I was in the same boat.

While not foolproof, Maxine's *modus operandi* worked well enough to get her into dozens of dance and rehearsal studios. After familiarizing herself with the studio and some of the people there, she would start to ask questions, ask about partners and who might be looking for a match-up:

> I'd tell them that I was looking for a partner and I'd put down names on a little list. I'd ask them for recommendations for another studio or I'd follow another girl to another studio.
> That's how I got my connections.
> If they knew a young man who was also looking for a partner, they'd say, "I'll call you."
> They would call me and I would go and try out with this particular young man whom they were suggesting.

Time and again Maxine would get a phone call to go and meet a prospective partner at a dance studio and try out, but the match-up was never right. For Maxine, it had to be more than just a good fit; it had to be perfect:

> It would be very nice. Usually he would be a very good dancer, but the spark wasn't there. I just didn't have any feeling. It wasn't right.
> He'd be too Latin or too jazzy or something.
> I didn't know what it was. All I knew was that the feeling wasn't there.
> I'd go to the next studio and it would be the same situation. I *still* didn't have the right feeling.

Again and again she was disappointed. Not one out of numerous potential match-ups produced the synergy that Maxine was seeking. After every failed attempt, Maxine would pack up her dance clothes and go back home, wondering if she would ever find the perfect partner:

> It was so discouraging. I almost gave up after more than two-dozen match-ups failed to furnish that magic spark to make a couple mesh.
> I was ready to quit.
> I had decided I would go back to modeling.

For a brief time she partnered with a dancer named Leonardo. They assembled a portfolio of professional photographs and auditioned for jobs, but they aroused only mild interest.

Then Maxine met Don Loper.

Maxine and Leonardo could not garner interest in their act.

My mother's best friend, who lived in England, was an actress. Her last name was Barrat. She was a top performer— and I always shot for the top.

In April 1937, Maxine was among hundreds of Hollywood hopefuls who entered their names and pictures in the *New York Evening Journal*'s "A Star is Born" contest sponsored by Selznick International Pictures. The event ran simultaneously with the opening at Radio City Music Hall of the film of the same name. A stunning headshot of Maxine was featured in the April 23, 1937 *Journal* article, "Gaynor Premiere Adds Many Entries to Film Contest," citing her as one of the beautiful girls selected as a semi-finalist for final judging on April 27th at the Radio City Music Hall Penthouse. The United Artists Pictures contest would be a prelude to future screen tests and a career as a Hollywood starlet.

Although Maxine had opportunities at social and charity engagements to dance professionally at some of New York's finer clubs, her career had yet to unfold. Maxine knew that she needed a partner to propel her to stardom, so she continued her search. While her father, who passed away on January 10, 1935, never lived to see Maxine's dreams come true, her mother reveled in all her daughter's many achievements right through Maxine's first appearance on television in December 1947. Monica Boura passed away on March 24, 1948, just prior to the debut of Maxine's first TV program, *And Everything Nice.*

Don Loper and Beth Hayes danced at Radio City Music Hall and other New York venues. In October 1936, they replaced the dance team of Maurine and Norva in the elegant Palm Room of the Hotel Commodore (later the New York Hyatt), which was renowned for big-style entertainment like Tommy Dorsey and his Orchestra. The following month Loper and Hayes were hired to complement the Eddie Elkins Orchestra at the newly renovated, magnificent Pall Mall Room at the Raleigh Hotel, the largest and grandest hotel in Washington, D.C. It proved to be quite a draw and fostered the hotel's reputation as a popular entertainment venue. The following fall they danced at the Savoy Hotel in London and reportedly toured Europe before breaking up their act. Thirty-year-old Don Loper booked passage as "Lincoln G. Loper" on the *S.S. Europa* departing from Southampton, England, and arrived in the port of New York on January 11, 1938.

In New York one of Maxine's friends told her about a very good dancer who had just returned from England. What's more, she told Maxine that he and his dance partner had split up—he was looking for a new partner. Maxine Recalls:

> A girlfriend of mine, who was a dancer in one of my classes, came to me and said, "Maxine, this chap has just come back to New York. He was dancing with this young lady and they broke up."

She had seen him dance with the other partner and she knew both of them very well. There was a conflict between them and they just couldn't make it together.

She said, "I know how hard you've tried, but will you *please* try out just one more time. I think you two would look great together. He'd be perfect for you."

Maxine jumped for joy when she finally found a partner!

Dancing with a Star

Maxine's reaction was guarded. After all, none of the leads that she had followed thus far had borne fruit. Why should this one be different? She was so discouraged by all the failed attempts, but her resolve never to give up spurred her to action. She would try one more time. They spoke:

> I told him that I was looking for a partner, and I'd heard that he was looking for one, too. I asked him if he wanted to try out together and see how it goes.
> "Well, ok," he said. "You need a partner and I need a partner, so let's give it whirl."
> We agreed to meet at a dance studio the next morning.

As arranged, they met at a local studio the following day. They went to their respective dressing spaces to change from their street clothes into dancing attire and emerged a few moments later ready to take their places.

The two dancers strode onto the studio dance floor, stopped at its center and turned toward one another. Their hands touched tentatively. As their eyes met, the phonograph needle was lowered onto a 78-rpm record. The music began.

Maxine Barrat took a step and Don Loper followed reflexively. Each time she moved, he moved in synch with her, again and again. Instantly it was apparent that there was a stunning dynamism—an incomparable synergy—between the dancers: *"We knew that was it."* It was a perfect match:

> I got into the studio with him and the minute the music started to play and I started to move, he started to move *just like I did.* From the minute we started to dance together, it was like magic.
> We took one look at each other and we both knew this was *so right.*
> It was like Ginger and Fred. With all the wonderful women dancers that Fred danced with after her, there was never the spark that he and Ginger had. It was the same thing with Don and me. We were just right for each other.
> I nearly fell over. I thought, my God, *this is it!*
> "Do you feel it, too?" I said.
> "Yes," he said.
> "This is it." I said.
> "Yes, this is it."
> It was wonderful.

PART II

LOPER & BARRAT

during the week of August 22nd and the production period got underway. The tryout was received very favorably by the public and played into September as one of the summer theater season's holdovers.

Some of the performers initially involved were: stage-screen actress

Maxine Barrat auditions for Village Barn.

Rose Hobart, best known for her role as Grazia in the 1929-30 Broadway production of *Death Takes a Holiday;* actress-singer Frances Comstock, who with Alfred Drake in Hamilton-Lewis' subsequent revue, *Two for the Show,* introduced "How High the Moon," which became an instant hit; British-American screen-stage actress Brenda Forbes, best remembered for a later trilogy (1980s) of TV movies in which she starred opposite Katharine Hepburn; actress-singer Patti Pickens, known with sisters Helen and Jane as the Pickens Sisters, a popular radio and recording vocal trio, who had the hit, "Did You Ever See a Dream Walking" (1934); and character actor Philip Bourneuf, who would have numerous stage credits before starting a long, successful film career.

In spite of the possibility of securing a part in a promising new theatrical production, Loper and Barrat remained jobless. They were getting desperate, knowing they wouldn't be able to hold out much longer. On the verge of giving up, they saw an ad in a trade newspaper for the Village Barn nightclub located in the basement of 52 West 8th Street in Greenwich Village. They knew their slick, sophisticated act was a mismatch for a country-music venue, but they also knew it might be their only chance to get a job and keep their dance act together. Loper and Barrat decided to speak with the club's owner, Meyer Horowitz:

> They were looking for a dance couple at the Village Barn. We thought, well, we need a job. So we went down there.
>
> Of course we didn't fit into the atmosphere very well because we were so sophisticated looking and the Village Barn was just that, a barn!

The Village Barn ("New York's Only Country Nite Club"), with three shows nightly (8 p.m.-11 p.m. and 2 a.m.), generally presented acts that fit into its hoedown atmosphere of corny music, zany novelty acts, square dancing and audience-participation games (hobbyhorse races, turtle races and so on). Typically, entertainers were attired in overalls and full gingham skirts, straw was scattered on the floor, a rooster was perched above the bandstand and club patrons sat at tables with clappers on both hands to express their approval. The rural-themed Village Barn was considered a "must" stop for out-of-towners, but not a place to go for fine entertainment. There were, however, a few notable performers who got their start there, including dancing-comedy vaudevillians-turned-Broadway performers, Paul Hartman and his wife Grace Barrett, stage-screen actress and radio comedienne Judy Canova and 1950s popular nightclub singer Don Cornell.

Village Barn owner Meyer Horowitz was perplexed by Loper and Barrat's plea to work at his cornpone club. They all knew the glossy dance act was not the right fit for his show. But when Loper and Barrat explained how badly they needed the work, Horowitz capitulated and decided to give them a break. He liked them and knew they had talent, so he offered them a job:

> We auditioned and the wonderful man that owned the Village Barn, Meyer Horowitz, said, "Well, you two don't belong here. Do you *really* need this job?"
> "Desperately," we said. "We're eating chocolate bars."
> So he put us in the show.

Loper and Barrat went into the Village Barn in mid-November as part of a show that included a musical comedy group called the Schnickelfritz band, acrobatic dancer Vera Fern, "veree Rooshian" singer Vira Niva, personable emcee-impressionist Johnny Howard and the Jack Sherr Orchestra. Billed as De la Penhas, Loper and Barrat were described by the *New York Times* as "a fast ballroom team with plenty of verve." *Variety* praised:

> Standing out in surrounding talent is the dance combo of Don Loper and Maxine Barrat, programmed as the De la Penhas, but who are introduced under their names. Two pertly-garbed dancers work easily. After opening ballroom number, a waltz with variations and a peppy Parisian conceit are employed as encores to vigorous returns.

After finishing their run at the Village Barn in December, Loper and Barrat joined the company of *One for the Money* for the out-of-town tryout before its Broadway premiere. The show had picked up the sponsorship of prominent Broadway producers Gertrude Macy and Stanley Gilkey in association with Robert F. Cutler and non-professional investors John Hay (Jock) Whiney and his sister, Mrs. Charles S. Payson, socialite patrons of the arts. Director-producer-songwriter-actor-screenwriter-lighting designer John Murray Anderson was chosen for staging the show. Major American dance choreographer Robert (Bob) Alton was selected to direct the dances and Edward Clarke Lilley, who had extensive theater credits, was tapped to stage the sketches. Future Tony award-winning Raoul Pène Du Bois, who would earn credits in 48 Broadway shows during his lifetime, was asked to design the sets and costumes:

When we first went into the show, I'll never forget this—this is typical Don. Robert Alton said, "I'll start your choreography tomorrow."

Don said, "*Nobody* does choreography for us. We do our own."

And this is our first show! I looked at him and thought, "Whoa!" Don was that way, very straightforward.

"Oh, well, all right," said Robert Alton. He was perfectly fine with it.

Then Don said, "However, you can criticize all you want. We will change according to your desire."

That settled it. He left us alone. He liked what he saw. We talked about it later, and I said, "I hope Don wasn't too abrupt." He said, "No, I understand that kind of thinking." He said he was very positive about what he feels is right. He had seen us, so he was aware of what we did—and we had auditioned for him, too.

"You two are so natural together. I assumed you'd come up with the right answer," he said.

In addition to Loper and Barrat, other performers retained from the September tryout were Brenda Forbes, Philip Bourneuf, Frances Comstock and baritone Alfred Drake, stage and future television star.

Other principals were signed: dancers Grace McDonald, Nadine Gae and Nell O'Day, a stage-and-screen star who had danced with Eleanor Powell in *Fine and Dandy* (1930); early television and stage character actor Keenan Wynn, who also would perform in Hamilton-Lewis' *Two for the Show;* and Ruth Matteson, Robert Smith, George Lloyd and (John) William Archibald, who according to Maxine, "was a *fabulous* dancer." He would later become known as a writer and for his adaptation of *The Turn of the Screw* for Broadway.

Also added to the cast of *One for the Money* was a young, little-known dancer named Gene Kelly, in what would be only his second Broadway appearance. Kelly had just left his Broadway debut role as a specialty dancer in Cole Porter's *Leave It to Me* (in which newcomer Mary Martin made Broadway history with her rendition of "My Heart Belongs to Daddy"). Luckily for Kelly, his agent Johnny Darrow was a friend of *Money*'s director John Murray Anderson; additionally, Bob Alton knew Kelly during his Pittsburgh years and as choreographer of *Leave It to Me.* Kelly was hired at twice the salary of

$115/week to act, sing and dance in eight of *One for the Money*'s 21 scenes. Maxine danced a short sequence with Gene Kelly in one scene.

It was the first time that Loper and Barrat met Gene Kelly. Known for his sardonic remarks, Don Loper made a prediction about Kelly's future as a dancer that not only would prove to be wrong but was one that he would never live down, according to Maxine:

York producers were sending one of the season's popular shows their way. The *Chicago Tribune* raved about the high caliber of the production despite its lack of a big-name cast, citing the superior talent of its youthful entertainers. Maxine recalled one night when things did not go as smoothly behind the scenes as it might have appeared to the audience:

> In one of the scenes Don and I made an entrance coming down a lighted stairway with a spotlight on us.
>
> We were going into the summer months and things were getting a little slower. They were trying to save some money, so they fired a few people. One was a stagehand and all he did in the *whole* show were two things: one was to put out a chair for one scene and the other was to plug in the light for us for our staircase.
>
> So Don said, "Well, that's nothing. I'll plug in the light."
>
> They said, "No, you can't." The union wouldn't let us put on a light on the staircase.
>
> We had to come down on a dark staircase because they wouldn't let us plug in that light. That, to me, was just *insane*. We had the big spotlight on us, of course, but that doesn't give you security like the lights of the stairway being lit properly.

Loper and Barrat's acclaimed performances in the New York and Chicago productions of *One for the Money* had created a buzz in theatrical circles. The duo had succeeded in getting the name, "Loper and Barrat," into the consciousness of Broadway professionals. It would not be long before producers would need a superlative dance team for a new musical production and it would be Loper and Barrat whom they would demand.

In New York new productions were being mounted for the upcoming fall 1939 theater season. Young Vincente Minnelli (later an Academy Award-winning film director, husband of Judy Garland and father of Liza Minnelli), who had been a Radio City Music Hall set designer and stage director and had worked on several Broadway shows, returned from a European trip and was ready to undertake a new project. One of Broadway's most successful producers, Max Gordon, hired him to design the sets, costumes and lighting as well as stage the production numbers for a new musical comedy to be called *Very Warm for May*. The book and lyrics were to be written by Oscar Hammerstein II, who would direct the book (staging), with music composed by Jerome Kern. Hammerstein-Kern were the much-revered team that had made Broadway history with *Show Boat*. *Very Warm for May* would be their first collaboration in many years; it also would be their final Broadway score.

The cast of Very Warm for May

In early October Loper and Barrat were engaged by Minnelli to perform a specialty dance number as Smoothy and Honey:

> Vincente Minnelli was a dreamy guy. We met him in the show and remained friends, going out to California and everything.
>
> He was so creative and had such a wonderful imagination—he was *always* dreaming up something. We dined together very often because we were friends, and we'd go out to dinner and he'd be designing something on the tablecloth or on a napkin. He'd be scribbling something right in the middle of dinner.
>
> He was full of ideas, which was so stimulating. Of course, Don and I loved that. So we had a lot in common.

A master of imagery, Minnelli set about designing his trademark extravagant scenery, dazzling costumes and special lighting effects to frame the elaborate musical production. He drew upon his boyhood memory of a barn in Delaware to create one of the principal sets about a barn's transformation into a summer theater. Acclaimed dancer-choreographer Albertina Rasch and Broadway veteran Harry Losee, who had worked with Minnelli on several other shows, were hired to direct the dances, but for the most part Loper and Barrat worked independently:

We did all our own choreography. We were given the music and made up our routine, fitting in with the show. If they didn't like something we had, they'd make another suggestion and we would switch according to what was best for the number.

The primary dances Don and I always did together. If I danced with anyone else, they were short dances that didn't amount to too much. He would dance with somebody and I would dance with somebody in a scene, but it didn't amount to anything.

Very Warm for May was a show within a show, about a society girl who flees from gangsters and hides out with a summer stock theater troupe, which is putting on a surrealistic avant-garde presentation. While *Very Warm for May* ultimately would fail, it introduced the quintessential Kern classic, "All the Things You Are," one of the most popular and enduring show tunes of all time. Ironically, Hammerstein never felt that the song—the centerpiece of the first act—would go anywhere, but it skyrocketed to success on the Hit Parade: Loper and Barrat danced in the elaborate scene of "All the Things You Are:"

Hollace Shaw [coloratura soprano], who had a beautiful, beautiful voice, sang "All the Things You Are," then we danced to it, melding one after the other.

Set designers labor long and hard to construct backdrops that create visual excitement and wow the audience. In the 1930s, '40s and '50s, Broadway stage performances were known for their elaborate sets.

Imagine while you are seated in a theater that you can view a snow-topped mountain shimmering in light cast from a huge overhead crystal chandelier hanging over this mountain. Enormous in size, the chandelier bulbs created thousands of sparkles on this man-made snowy mountain.

The set design was very elaborate and the mountain was very high. From the front it looked so, so gorgeous, with the lighting effect and everything. The ceiling of the set reached five office-building stories high. The ceiling high mountain was constructed with a hidden staircase at the back. Naturally you couldn't see the built-in stairway from out front; you couldn't see the steps. Every performance, Don and I climbed the towering steps set to the top of the mountain and waited for our cue.

and critics applauded the brisk pace of dancing and singing, the elaborate sets and fine acting. Loper and Barrat's performance was among those most highly praised and given special mention in *Variety*: "Harry Losee's dances, both specialty and ballet, scored heavily."

The underlying problems and confusion with the book worsened after producer Max Gordon showed up shortly before the Wilmington tryout. Gordon had been in Hollywood for the filming of his hit play, *Abe Lincoln in Illinois* (1938) and absent for the preparation and most of the production of *Very Warm for May*. When he arrived on the scene, he was aghast at the show's weaknesses and demanded drastic revisions. By the time the show had finished out-of-town tryouts in Philadelphia and Boston, it had been rewritten completely. Howard Losee had been dismissed and Max Gordon had brought in Hassard Short, renowned as an at-large-musical-comedy-production "doctor," as a consultant replacing Minnelli:

> Vincente Minnelli directed the show for part of the time—he directed it up to a point. There were differences of opinion and it was decided to have somebody come in and direct it to take it to Broadway. Vincente Minnelli left prior to its going to Broadway.
>
> It was such a good show, but they kept changing it and changing it so many times that we didn't know what end was up. When we were up in Boston, they took out a whole number.
>
> It was such a shame.

The ballyhoo and anticipation of a long-awaited Hammerstein-Kern collaboration changed to disappointment when a badly doctored *Very Warm for May* opened at the Alvin Theatre, November 17, 1939. *Variety* criticized the show's ponderous, shapeless plot, "...it's all such a confused jumble." While the stunning scenery, colorful costumes, singing and dancing received high marks, it was the lambasted book that brought the show to its knees.

Amid the wreckage, however, some highly memorable performances emerged. Critic Robert Coleman, who was in the audience at the Alvin on the night of November 17, 1939, recognized Loper and Barrat's show-stopping performance and contribution to musical theater: "Don Loper and Maxine Barrat, one of our top-flight ballroom teams...set the first-nighters acheering."

Maxine and Don on stage at Loew's State Theatre

The unfortunate fate of *Very Warm for May* was best summarized by its musical arranger Russell Bennett as "a great show that was produced into a failure," or, as it came to be called by Eve Arden, *Very Cold for October*. Even with the wealth of talent backstage and on, the show could not be saved. *Very Warm for May* closed January 6, 1940 after holding on through the traditionally lucrative Christmas and New Year's Day holidays. Although the show had failed, Loper and Barrat had triumphed: "Don Loper and Maxine Barrat repeat the success they achieved last year as a dance team in *One for the Money*," hailed the *New York World-Telegraph*.

Shortly after the show's final curtain at the Alvin, Loper and Barrat were tapped to appear in a variety show at the Loew's State Theatre, 1540 Broadway (now Bertelsmann office tower). The last vaudeville house in Times Square by 1940, Loew's State was one of Manhattan's grand movie palaces that competed for major film world-premiere revenues and offered popular variety shows between movie showings.

Host of the Loew's State staged event, opening Thursday, January 18, 1940, was Louis Sobol, Broadway personality and *Journal-American* columnist. As master of ceremonies, Sobol presented beloved comedian and big box-office draw Joe E. Lewis, model-actress Cobina Wright, Jr. (whose name made news headlines the previous year when she sued Bob Hope for using her as the basis for a character on his radio show), harmonica act Jimmy and Mildred Mulcay, the tap dancing Sinclair Sisters and Loper and Barrat.

Loper and Barrat met Joe E. Lewis for the first time when they shared the bill with him at their Loew's State debut:

> Joe E. Lewis was a friend of ours. He was fun. He was a jewel. We had a lot of good times with him, mostly lunches or dinners, nothing special, just wonderful companionship.
>
> He was a very big star, one of the biggest at the time. He deserved to be. He was fabulous. People just loved him. He could do no wrong. He was *so* good, and he'd come out with these off-the-cuff remarks. A couple of times he engaged me in his routine and we would have some fun lines together. I never knew what he was going to do next! One time I chided him, 'You're ruining my dignity!' I just went along with whatever happened and we made it up as we went along. With him it was easy to do. We were good pals.
>
> He was the same offstage. He was always clowning around. You would go to dinner with him and you'd be laughing all through dinner with his crazy remarks. He was great fun to be with.

The week beginning Thursday, February 22, 1940 brought the realization of a dream for Maxine when Loper and Barrat starred in *Curtain Time* at Radio City Music Hall—the Showplace of the Nation—where Maxine had spent so many hours watching her idol Ginger Rogers dance with Fred Astaire on the theater's huge screen. As was customary for much of the theater's history, both a film and a stage show were presented as part of the same program. At the time there were five showings a day of the RKO film, *Abe Lincoln in Illinois*, starring Raymond Massey and Howard DaSilva, who recreated on screen their roles in the original Broadway show, both produced by Max Gordon.

Loper and Barrat

Maxine wore a frothy pink dress for "All the Things You Are" at Radio City Music Hall.

Due to the long running time of the film, it was a slightly abbreviated stage show with four components: "Harlequinade," an original ballet set to music by Richard Drigo, that was specially choreographed by the director of the Music Hall Corps de Ballet Florence Rogge and featured dancers Paul Haakon, Leda Anchutina, Nicholas Daks and Louise Fornaca; "A Sentimental Mood," featuring Loper and Barrat, Earl Lippy and the Music Hall Glee Club; "Gay Moments," with a vaudeville band-imitation trio known as the Three Oxford Boys; and

"Rhumba," with Loper and Barrat, Robert Regent and Hilda Eckler, followed by Loper and Barrat ushering in the line of colorfully costumed Rockettes, who performed a Latinized routine incorporating their famous kicks and spectacular precision work.

Loper and Barrat's appearance during the Glee Club's performance of "A Sentimental Mood" was brief, but noteworthy. "Earl Lippy solos with the group while the dance duo of Loper and Barrat gets scarcely more than a couple of minutes to peddle its wares, but shows considerable smoothness and some neat twirls and lifts," declared *Variety*. "Both members are very acceptable lookers, too."

Wearing a frothy pink dress, Maxine was then lowered on a pink cloud-platform from the ceiling to the stage floor while the Radio City Music Hall all-male glee club sang "All the Things You Are." While the opportunity thrilled Maxine, the logistics of the act terrified her:

> We were asked to appear at Radio City Music Hall. I thought it was tone of the most beautiful places in the world.
>
> The height from the ceiling to the Great Stage is equivalent to several stories in a commercial office building. They decided to lower me on a pink cloud from the ceiling to the stage while a chorus of men sang the beautiful, romantic lyrics of "All the Things You Are" from *Very Warm for May*.
>
> They would lower me to the stage and Don would be there with the 36 men who were singing "All the Things You Are." Don would step out of that group, come over and lift me up off the pink cloud and we would do our dance number.
>
> It was all very lovely and romantic, except for one thing. I'm afraid of heights!
>
> Three times a day I shivered coming down on that cloud and four to five times a day on Saturdays and Sundays.
>
> Needless to say, I was very happy when that engagement ended; however, I was very grateful to have been at the wonderful Radio City Music Hall.

DANCE FASHIONISTS DELIGHT AUDIENCES

We nominate for international acclaim the "dance team of the year" . . . Don Loper and Maxine Barrat! One of the most graceful yet one of the oddest duos in the country.

Spread largely by word of mouth, news of their splendid performance reached entertainment seekers and venue operators alike. It wasn't long before Loper and Barrat received an offer to appear at the Hotel New Yorker on a bill with the Al Donahue Orchestra with Pauline Kelly and comedian Giovanni. The legendary

Hotel New Yorker was built in the same art deco-style as the Empire State Building and the Chrysler Building, all within close proximity in midtown Manhattan. The New Yorker was known for presenting top-notch bands and supporting floor shows. *Variety* called Loper and Barrat "a class ballroom team who've been around, but heretofore not specially 'noticed'." Their opening bolero arrangement of "Night and Day" and lively "I Know That You Know" were regarded as "unusual in execution," a tribute to their inventiveness. It was a testament to their growing presence on the entertainment scene that they received their first New Acts review in the same *Variety,* April 3, 1940 issue:

> Class couple, he in tails and the blonde vis-à-vis in slick and sleek hair-do, make a fine appearance on the floor. Their terps verge on the ballet, and in fact some of their stuff was adagio in the past. However here they utilize that training to excellent advantage with some unusual holds and lifts, calling for expert balance and much strength on his part, although done with suavity and ease. They fit any café floor show mass or class.

Loper and Barrat were becoming known for the thrill and entertainment value that they brought to shows, which largely accounted for their next recruitment: a third and final appearance in a Broadway show, *All in Fun*. The musical revue originally consisted of material by a dozen or more individuals and co-starred Phil Baker and Leonard Sillman, with specialties by Bill ("Bojangles") Robinson, Imogene Coca, Pert Kelton, Rosita Moreno, Red Marshall, Wynn Murray and others.

During its premiere on November 21, 1940 at the Shubert Theatre in New Haven, a four-performance break-in, it became apparent that *All in Fun* was beset with internal strife and there were serious flaws with the production. After it opened in Boston, several principals opined that its producer Leonard Sillman, in his first big effort, should step aside in favor of someone more experienced. Sillman agreed to enlist the help of several production "doctors" and hired veteran John Murray Anderson to restage the show. Lee Shubert suggested that *All in Fun* be kept out of town for another six weeks, but backers were unwilling to provide additional funding for a show in which they had already invested approximately $90,000. Phil Baker, whose role in *All in Fun* marked his return to the stage after a six-year hiatus, co-produced and invested heavily in it, but dropped out a week before its scheduled Broadway opening. Loper and Barrat were brought in as one of the last-ditch efforts to save the show.

Bill Robinson, the much-loved tap dancing genius, was billed as the star of *All in Fun* when it opened on Friday night, December 27, 1940 at the Majestic Theatre. Loper and Barrat danced with other members of the cast to "Love and I" sung by Walter Cassel, and they were featured in a solo routine to "How Did It Get So Late So Early?" as performed by Marie Nash. *The New York Times* declared, "Don Loper and Maxine Barrat dance better than you realize…"

Overnight the show closed. "'All in Fun' Expires Abruptly" declared the *New York Times*, reporting that *All in Fun* had closed after one preview and three local showings. The show had brought in only $6,900 against approximately $125,000 in production costs that included the three-and-a-half week tryout losses at New Haven and Boston.

Despite the failure of *All in Fun*, Loper and Barrat's reputation as innovative performing artists continued to grow. One press agent by the name of Mary Anita Loos, in particular, had taken a special interest in this up-and-coming dance team. Loos, who was the niece of writer Anita Loos (*Gentlemen Prefer Blondes*) and had her own public relations firm in New York at the time, was working for the Copacabana nightclub, a new entertainment establishment that had opened in late October. The Copa's floorshow needed a lift—new energy—to bring in the crowds and "make the cash register sing," as Copa operator Jules Podell famously used to say. Mary Anita Loos had a fresh idea of how to make that happen.

During the early months of 1941, Loos would propose to Copa owner Monte Proser a plan that would put both the Copacabana and Loper and Barrat on a trajectory to world fame.

Chapter Eight
The World-Famous Copacabana

An impeccable dresser, Don Loper had an artistic eye and a flair for fashion. After the breakup of Loper and Barrat in the mid-'40s, he went on to become world famous as a Hollywood couturier to the stars.

While still partnering with Maxine, he operated a successful dress shop in New York and designed clothing for an exclusive clientele that included only those personalities that interested him, such as American stage legend Katharine Cornell and Ginger Rogers. Known for his acerbic wit and haughtiness, Don Loper once remarked: "I turn away enough business to make it interesting. Trouble is most women don't dress their personalities; they follow a fad. If Ginger Rogers wears it, they want it."

Loper resided in a beautifully appointed, candle-lit apartment located at the top of a rickety staircase accessed through a tenement door on Lexington Avenue on New York's East Side. Maxine lived at her parent's home on East 235th Street in the Bronx. The dancers had a platonic relationship throughout their partnership; they remained friends long after they broke up as a professional dance team.

From the outset Loper created a look for Maxine that was a stylemark of their partnership, inspiring admiring looks both on and off the dance floor. Maxine was the first member of a dance team to wear a hat and long gloves as part of a fashionable, sophisticated look:

> Don made all my clothes. His designs were so beautiful. He was a fabulous designer and I *loved* his creations.

Suave, dark-haired Don Loper, whose facial features and expressions resembled those of actor Danny Kaye, and lovely, blonde Maxine Barrat were creating a buzz around town for both their remarkable dancing and exquisite fashion styling. Then-publicist Mary Anita Loos believed that the multi-talented Loper and Barrat could bring elegance and verve, along with dynamite box office and press, to Manhattan's newest hotspot and one of her clients, the Copacabana, at 10 East 60th Street.

The Depression was waning and a world war was looming. These were the halcyon days of entertainment. Nightclubs were booming.

The top nightclubs were sophisticated, elegant and studded with all the little touches that added sparkle to living during those years. Many of these Gotham institutions were Prohibition speakeasies reborn as elegant restaurants following the repeal in 1933. They became the famous New York swinging "in" places of the day: the Colony, the aristocratic 21 Club; John Perona's plush and sophisticated El Morocco (with its zebra-skin motif); and its rival, Sherman Billingsley's homey Stork Club, which billed itself as the early 1940s' "swank spot." Other nightspots combined the club atmosphere of these "swell joints," which were dominantly eateries rather than niteries, with entertainment: Kit Kat Club, Hurricane, Havana-Madrid, La Martinique, Diamond Horseshoe and so many others. The many jazz clubs on "Swing Street," 52nd Street between Fifth and Sixth Avenues, were also popular: the Onyx, "88," Club 18 and Leon & Eddie's (later Toots Shors).

To bring in the crowds nightclubs and restaurants hired press agents to beat the drum to promote their clients. By 1942, New York City's top 50-crystal-and-chromium establishments were competing for revenues that yielded a gross profit of more than $85 million a year.

Press agents came into being as a result of the need for gossip by Broadway columnists, who in turn, provided a newspaper editor with unreliable but edition-selling "items" about stars of the stage and screen as well as café society gadabouts. Tremendous pressure was brought to bear on newspapers by advertisers, chiefly restaurants and

Man About Manhattan
By George Tucker

NEW YORK — Copacabana is a Portuguese word with no literal meaning, yet to those who know Rio it means soft lights and romance; it means white dinner jackets and beautiful women; it means murmuring trade winds and white hot stars hanging low over the blue velvet harbor of Rio de Janeiro.

Actually Copacabana is one of the beach districts of Rio—an exclusive and well bred district in the sense that Hyde Park or Edgewater beach is exclusive. Break the word down, and you have copa, meaning cup; and cabana, meaning house. Put them together and they mean nothing that can be translated into English.

* * *

WE WERE a little concerned about this because Copacabana is also a new night club in New York. It is on East 60th street in an old basement of a hotel—a basement that stood empty and abandoned for more than ten years. It was here that Rudy Vallee augmented his fame 12 years ago and founded the Villa Vallee; a popular spot back in the days when F. Scott Fitzgerald was the hero of the flapper age and college boys wore coonskin coats.

We want to tell you a little about this club because it has the odd distinction of being in good taste. Its color scheme is white, rust, and green. White is important this year.

This basement is supported by several large hideous posts. When Monte Proser, who owns the club, inspected it, he sent for Clark Robinson, the lean, moustached, gray-templed scenic designer who designed all the Translux theaters in New York.

nightclubs, to report the comings and goings of their celebrated clientele. The press agent was poised between the proprietor, whose establishment just *had* to be mentioned in the columns, and the gossip columnist, who was long on stories but short on space. A publicist's power is illustrated by the following account by Abner Klipstein, press agent for the Shuberts:

> When I was the acting press agent for the Shuberts, I'd walk around from theater to theater. I'd run into press agents for other attractions and we'd arrange to meet later. We'd say, "Let's go to the Copacabana for a drink," or Leon & Eddie's, the Rainbow Room, Lindy's. The Copa was a short walk over to the East Side from Broadway. The first time we went there, we wanted to see it because it was new.
>
> The maître d' put us at a table. We had a drink, watched the show and we recognized some of the girls who'd been in Broadway shows.
>
> When we got up to leave, we asked for a check.
>
> The maitre d' said, "There's no check."
>
> I guess it was because we were press agents and they figured that we might say something that would get in the paper—slip an item to Walter Winchell, Louis Sobol, Dorothy Kilgallen, Dan Walker, Ed Sullivan, Earl Wilson, Leonard Lyon. There were so many newspapers—the *Graphic*, the *News*, the *Mirror*—and every one had a Broadway columnist, or two, or three.
>
> It was a thriving business, and entertainers and nightclubs were *very* conscious of publicity. It was their lifeblood.

A former publicity agent for Mary Pickford, Hedy Lamarr, Lupe Velez and others, as well as owner of such successful nightclubs as La Conga (Hollywood)

and the Beachcomber, Copa owner Monte Proser strove to maintain a reputation for being on the cutting edge of nightclub offerings. His ambition was to make the Copacabana the most famous nightclub in the world. At the time it was rumored that Proser wanted to make some changes in his show, perhaps replace the current dance team of Estelle and Leroy. His press agent Mary Anita Loos offered some advice.

Dancing with a Star

Loos proposed that Proser hire Loper and Barrat, not only for their appeal as one of New York's hottest up-and-coming dance teams but also for their potential to create, develop and stage future shows. Loper and Barrat could hold the key for charting a fresh course that would take the Copacabana to new heights of fame and fortune, Loos argued. "Why don't you give them a chance, Monte?" As it turned out, he did—and she was right.

Monte Proser brought them into a show in April 1941, according to Maxine:

> The Copa was already established. It was a dream to go into the Copa. It was the top nightclub in the world.
>
> The Copa was very elegant in those days. You couldn't even get into the Copa if you weren't dressed in dinner clothes.
>
> Here we were unknown really, and they *always* had somebody well known at the Copa. We went there to do one night. That one night, of course, was our big break.

Loper and Barrat appeared on a bill with torch songstress Bernice Parks, who was held over from the previous show, along with long-standing Copa emcee-singer Fernando Alvares. Formerly a vocalist with the Russ Morgan Orchestra, Bernice Parks had been recruited from the West Coast version of the stage show *Meet the People*. Also on the bill was Latin American singing idol Juan Arvizu, the "Bing Crosby of South America," who had come to America under contract with Columbia Broadcasting Company. Other attractions were actress-singer Nina Orla, former soloist with the Xaviar Cugat Orchestra and film actress (*Where Did You Get That Girl?* and Universal Studio's low-budget hit *Buck Privates*, starring Abbott and Costello); the Nat Brandwynne and Frank Marti orchestras, which supplied the music for the show and the dancing; and the Broadway-doubling Samba Sirens (later called Copa Girls).

Plaza 8-1060

Jules Podell's
copacabana
10 East 60th Street · New York

The shows (8 p.m., 12 midnight and 2 a.m.) were directed and produced by former vaudeville and Broadway dancer Billy Reed, who went on to open his Little Club after the war. Grace Gillern, then 22 and doubling in Irving Berlin's *Louisiana Purchase*, was one of the original Samba Sirens in the first Copa line; she described the club's early days and the big draw of interpretive and exhibition ballroom teams in those years:

> On opening night [October 31, 1940], you could feel the electricity in the air. We *knew* we had something wonderful going on. It was *very* exciting. The house was packed, *packed.*

Dancing with a Star

Winchell, everybody, just *raved* about the show and the girls and the performers.

There were no big stars at the Copa then. What brought in the crowds were the singers and the dance teams and the girls.

On April 23, 1941, the dance team of Loper and Barrat took a Copa audience by surprise and brought down the house in the second show. While some critics raved about their fundamental technical skill, others claimed the dance team's strong appeal lay in their exquisite coloring of dance movements. Everyone agreed, however, that Loper & Barrat brought an unparalleled intensity to the story they were telling. "All of our dances start with an idea," Don Loper once said of their original, even unorthodox, approach to their routines. "For instance, it might be a flirtation, or two old friends meeting or a scene between lovers."

Their opening night at the Copacabana was one of the most magical moments of their career, Maxine vividly recalled:

The night came and we were very excited, very nervous, but we went on and did the first show, which went very nicely.

By the 12 o'clock show, the place was jam-packed. We were very tentative; however, we went out, did two numbers, took our bow and went off. The audience was applauding so we came back out, took another bow and went off. They were *still* applauding. We went back, bowed, and they still applauded.

The audience *loved* us. We stopped the show!

So Don took the microphone and he said: "Ladies and gentlemen. Thank you so much for this warm welcome. We just came back from London—and he looked at me with a twinkle in his eye. We only had time to rehearse two numbers. Please come back. We'd be delighted to dance for you."

And off he came.

You can *imagine* how we felt. I burst into tears. He burst into tears. The rest of the cast all around us were applauding and saying, "You've made it! You really made it!"

We *knew* that we had—and we knew that life would never be the same—*and it surely wasn't.*

Overnight they became the must-see sensation at the newest and smartest nightclub in New York. Their names moved up in the billing, headlining with Bernice Parks. The breakthrough performance of Loper and Barrat was the latest talk of the town. Monte Proser wanted nothing more than to capitalize on their spectacular success and sign them for an extended return engagement in the fall. He offered them a contract to reopen the club after the summer hiatus and

stay on to star in the Copacabana's first anniversary show on October 31, 1941. In the meantime, talent agents were clamoring to represent this dynamite dance team that was taking New York by storm:

> Right away the agents wanted to sign us. We said, "No, we don't want to sign." It was so stupid, of course, but they had turned us down so many times. Monte Proser said, "Come on,

Dancing with a Star

kids, you've got to sign with them [William Morris Agency] because they do our whole show." So that's how we happened to sign with them.

News of their stunning performance spread throughout the dance world, piquing widespread interest. Ginger Rogers, actress and dancing partner to Fred Astaire, got wind of this so-called hot new dance team that was the talk of New York City; she decided to go to the Copa to see firsthand what all the fuss was about. The famed dancer invited Don

Maxine visits Ginger Rogers' ranch.

Loper and Maxine Barrat to her ringside table after the show, and Maxine finally met her teenage idol. They struck up an immediate friendship.

Here's the interesting thing about our meeting. You know how you meet a lot of people in life, but every once in a great while you meet somebody and you know you're going to be friends forever? So rare. That happened to us.

As I sat down and said, "Hello,"... it was remarkable because with dancers, usually there's jealousy. But there was none of that, for her or for me.

She felt the same way. The two of us looked at each other and we just knew. We just knew. It was the strangest, most wonderful moment and it's so hard to relate that to anybody. It was so tender and so beautiful, so all knowing. We just knew as though maybe we'd been friends

Ginger and Maxine

somewhere else. It was almost as if we picked up where we had left off—and we both felt it! We looked at each other and just knew we'd be friends forever—and, of course, we were—until she passed on.

It was such a thrill because I had been going to Radio City Music Hall and watching her every move. I would sit there all

Ginger Rogers (left) and Maxine Barrat (right) each found a soul mate for life when they first met.

day long at Radio City Music Hall just to see her come out and dance again. That night, I started to tell her about it. Once I felt that complete connection, I felt I had to tell her how long I had been her admirer and she didn't know it! She felt good about hearing it, and she was just so great.

She said, "I thought we had a connection!"

The fact that she felt it too to me was remarkable, because it was the last thing in the world that I expected. I thought I'd be so in awe of her that there wouldn't be a connection like there was that very moment.

We talked about careers. Her career. My career, and the potential for my career. Right away she started giving me ideas about what I could do, Don and I.

Ginger was in New York visiting friends, seeing Broadway shows and so forth. She was on holiday. She had very dear friends in New York who were with her at the table that night. There were about six people.

We talked between shows. We had another show coming up, so we probably sat there for about 20 minutes. Then we knew we had to go and do another show. We thanked her very much. In the meantime, we traded phone numbers and addresses.

She said, "You must keep in touch."

I said, "You bet we will!"

From that time on, we stayed in touch. We remained close until Ginger's death in 1995.

As newly feted celebrities, Loper and Barrat became fodder for New York newspaper gossipmongers, whose attention-grabbing items circulated coast-to-coast in syndicated columns. Items unreliable but printable titillated readers' imaginations, such as Walter Winchell's mention in his *New York Daily Mirror* column: "Edmund

Ginger Rogers and Maxine remained friends 'til the end.

Lowe [vaudeville, silent film and Hollywood actor] and Maxine Barrat, the Copa dancer, are togethering a lot. Chums say she reminds him of his first wife, Lilyan Tashman...."

While there was a connection in name only, a successful turn at Copacabana New York landed Loper and Barrat an offer to dance at the world-class Copacabana Palace Hotel in Rio de Janeiro. When their triumphant stand at the Copa ended in May, Loper and Barrat set off for the

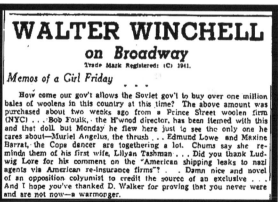

WALTER WINCHELL

on Broadway

Trade Mark Registered: (C) 1941.

Memos of a Girl Friday ...

How come our gov't allows the Soviet gov't to buy over one million bales of woolens in this country at this time? The above amount was purchased about two weeks ago from a Prince Street woolen firm (NYC) ... Bob Foulk, the H'wood director, has been itemed with this and that doll, but Monday he flew here just to see the only one he cares about—Muriel Angelus, the thrush ... Edmund Lowe and Maxine Barrat, the Copa dancer are togethering a lot. Chums say she reminds them of his first wife, Lilyan Tashman ... Did you thank Ludwig Lore for his comment on the "American shipping leaks to nazi agents via American re-insurance firms"? . . Damn nice and novel of an opposition colyumist to credit the source of an exclusive . . . And I hope you've thanked D. Walker for proving that you never were and are not now—a warmonger.

social whirl of the most vibrant capital of the world at the time, fabulous Rio.

Chapter Nine
"Tico Tico no Fubá"

In his 1933 inaugural address, President Franklin D. Roosevelt had embraced the Good Neighbor Policy on behalf of our country, which rekindled an interest in Latin culture that had begun in the 1920s with the popularity of silent film's Rudolph Valentino, dubbed Hollywood's "Latin Lover." Latin music conjured up the romance and joie de vivre of festive Rio de Janeiro, a popular winter destination for fashionable New Yorkers. Dances like the conga, samba and rhumba were hot, and ballroom dance teams were very popular at Rio's nightspots. At the time, the then-Brazilian capital's glamorous nightlife was divided among the elegant Copacabana district's famous casinos: the showy Copacabana, belonging to the Copacabana Palace Hotel—the large and gaudy Cassino da Urca—where Carmen Miranda was discovered by Lee Shubert—and the Cassino Atlantico, with its line of lovely, beautifully costumed American girls. The floor shows at these café society nightclubs primarily featured chorus and vaudeville acts from the United States. Well-to-do cosmopolitan Brazilians in dinner jackets, or bejeweled and gowned, danced the samba to the music provided by popular orchestras like Eddy Duchin.

With its stunning Atlantica Avenue location on the long, crescent-shaped Copacabana beach overlooking the sea, the stucco-fashioned, neoclassical Copacabana Palace Hotel had played host to Rio's high society, royalty, world and business leaders, as well as stars of stage, film, music and sports since the opening of its art deco doors in 1923. Designed by French architect

Postcard from Copacabana Palace Hotel in Rio

Dancing with a Star

Joseph Gire and owned by the Guinle family of Rio de Janeiro, the sumptuous Copacabana Palace was known to the American public as the setting for the breakthrough film *Flying Down to Rio* starring Fred Astaire and Ginger Rogers.

Composer-pianist Dave Dreyer, Maxine and Don relax on their way to South America.

Standing at the ship's rail on their way to Rio, Don Loper and Maxine Barrat daydreamed of following in the footsteps of Astaire and Rogers and dancing on the lustrous floors of the luxurious Copacabana Palace:

> When we were finished at the Copacabana and the season was pretty much over in New York, we were invited to go to the Copacabana in Rio—and *that* was an extraordinary experience.
>
> They had other acts. We were one of the acts. It was a regular nightclub show, all nightclub performers.
>
> It was *wonderful*.
>
> We carried our own music with us to fit our routines and we had orchestrations made up. We had a *wonderful* orchestra. They loved us, so they were with us all the way.
>
> It was a *beautiful* adventure.

The team of Loper and Barrat was a smash at the Copacabana Palace as well as at the Grill Room of the Cassino Atlantico, one of the top venues for popular acts of the day. Although they had been brought in to augment holdovers Agustin Lara, Ana Maria Gonzalez and Geraldine Dubois, the originality and elegance of the exciting new dance team from the United States pleased the enthusiastic capacity crowds as much as, if not more than, the headliners. A picture of Don Loper and Maxine Barrat appeared in a local Rio newspaper, with the headline:

Crowds Nightly in the Grill Room of The Casino Atlantico
Agustin Lara, Ana Maria Gonzalez, Loper and Barrat, Geraldine and Joe, Juliana Yanakaiva and the Glamour Girls form Show which is Breaking Records in Rio's Favorite Boite

The article went on to say, "…seconding the star act is the new dance team of Loper and Barrat. The dancing of this young couple has captivated the audience

as have the costumes worn by Miss Barrat. These costumes are designed by her partner and have attracted attention wherever the act has appeared."

Rio was a swiftly revolving social scene, from its fine dining in the spacious rooms of the Copacabana, fancy-dress cocktail parties and ballroom lessons on the polished floors of the Atlantico and Urca clubs, to its top-notch entertainment at the district's finest nightspots. For Loper and Barrat it was an opportunity to luxuriate in the cultural riches of South America, inspiring them to grow artistically. They were awed by the wealth of material offered by the folklore—in particular, the native music, rhythms and folk dances with their potential for innovative choreographic applications for American audiences. It was at this time that Loper and Barrat developed their unique and advant-garde style of integrating native South American steps into their routine that made them stand out from the typical glossy ballroom styles of other café performers of the day.

The dance team that had won over New York with their extraordinary performances was unprepared, however, for the audience's reaction on their opening night:

The place itself was magnificent, of course. The hotel was right on the waterfront. Even the sidewalks are all paved with gorgeous colors and everything. It's just a beautiful place. We were in this wonderful hotel called the Copacabana.

Our opening night was a party for the president [Getúlio Vargas]. The place was jammed to the rafters. I had on one of my best dresses, with the jewelry and the whole bit.

We'd rehearsed in the afternoon. We had had a wonderful rehearsal, although we couldn't speak the language, but the guys who were playing for us just felt our tempo and we felt their music, and it was good. We felt very comfortable.

That night we came out to dance, and while we're dancing, *there isn't one sound in the whole place. Nothing.* At the Copa [New York] you always hear the sound of someone moving a foot, or somebody moving around or something happening. You hear little noises when you're performing. Not much, but you hear something. Here, there wasn't one sound. It was like there was nobody there. We went through our numbers, and when we were finished, they went, "Boo. Sssss."

They're sissing and they're stamping their feet and they're booing and sissing and stamping. And *the shock*—Don and I stood there. I burst into tears, and we ran off stage.

We didn't know that *that* was their way of applauding! Nobody told us. We could have killed them up at the William Morris office. We said to them, "You should have *told us.* You wrecked our performance."

After we had run off stage, we said to each other, "We can't be *that* bad!" We had had all these accolades from everybody in New York and now we come here and they're booing us.

But that was their way of applauding.

Finally someone came out and said, "Go, mor [sic], mor. Go, go. Mor, mor."

Then we realized—we finally went back out. By then the mascara is running and the tears. We were both shaken. Of course, you come through. We got our equilibrium back to be able to carry on. That took some doing. But the music played and we did some more numbers—we danced some more for them.

COPACABANA BEACH

But, *my God*, I have never been so shocked in my whole life.

The *enormity* of a dead silence—and then this booing and shushing, hissing and the stamping of the feet. We were scared to death because we thought we were terrible. In our way of thinking we were terrible, but to their way of thinking, we were wonderful.

That was one of the toughest nights we ever had—to get our equilibrium back and carry on.

For Maxine the five-week stay in Rio was a wonderful, unique adventure, filled with offstage—as well as onstage—surprises:

I had the most amazing experiences there. Like everything else, their way of doing things is quite different.

There was a gentleman who took a fancy to me. I didn't know it, of course; we didn't know it. He would sit in the foyer of the hotel and watch me go by. He finally found somebody who knew somebody who knew us. He gave a party, so that we could meet.

He and I started to go out together a few times. The next thing you know, I get a knock at the door of my hotel room one morning. And here come three men with trays of jewelry. I was

Dancing with a Star

Loper and Barrat perform at Radio City Music Hall prior to their Rio appearance. (Photo by Jimmy Sileo)

to pick out anything I wanted. There were rubies, emeralds, sapphires—all these jewels!

That's the way they do things.

I looked at them and I said, "I can't accept any of these jewels. Thank him very much; it's very sweet." I sent them all back.

So then, he started to send me—since I wouldn't take jewels—beautiful pocketbooks and a few things like that. That was all right, but I wasn't about to take diamonds.

Then he said, "I'd like to do something for you and Don because you're such a hit here, and everybody loves you so much." So he sent over three different types of cars. We could use any of those cars—just pick a car that you like, he said, and you can drive around any place you want to for your whole stay here. We took one car, a convertible, and we had fun driving around in it.

He followed me to the United States afterwards. I told him, "I can't become involved because I owe my partner my

Lela Rogers poses with her soon-to-be-famous daughter Ginger.

they had a shower. They were showered to get rid of the flies that had collected on their bodies. Lela designed that herself.

Lela lived there a good portion of the time, but never full-time because she had her own apartment in L.A.

Lucille Ball said, "behind every successful actress are a hairdresser and a mother," and she described Mrs. Lela E. Rogers as "the mother of all mothers." Lela was the hard-driving powerhouse advocate behind the Ginger Rogers success story. Maxine says:

> Ginger was an only child. Her father left them before she was born. Her mother raised her, supported her, encouraged her, absolutely. Lela deserves a lot of credit. Without her, I think Ginger would have had a tough time trying to make it.
>
> Lela was a writer; she was a journalist. Without her mother, Ginger would never have made it, I don't think, because Ginger was a little bit timid when she was young. She got more secure as she got more successful. Her mother was the one who broke the ice. She gave her all these wonderful things to say when

she was doing an audition or whatever. Ginger would have something clever to say, to make her stand out. It all helped with her getting attention. A natural dancer, but she also had all these snappy remarks to make—that was all her mother. Lela did all the negotiations for her contracts—*everything.*

They were very close.

Ginger was born Virginia Katherine McMath on July 16, 1911 in Independence, Missouri, Ginger's father left her mother before Ginger was born. As a youngster Ginger temporarily resided with her maternal grandparents in Kansas City, while her mother supported her as a Hollywood scriptwriter. After her mother's marriage in 1920 to John Rogers (whom Ginger adored and whose name she used although she was never legally adopted by him), the family lived in Texas. Vaudeville was in its heyday. The top acts of the day—George Burns and Gracie Allen, Jack Benny and his wife Sadie (Marks), Eddie Foy, George Jessel, Sophie Tucker and others—played Texas theaters on the big circuits. Silent film stars such as Gloria Swanson and Rudolph Valentino also traveled to these movie houses to promote their latest movies. At an early age Ginger Rogers was impressed by the lavish fanfare that accompanied film premieres. Women were dressed to the nines in elegant evening clothes, diamond adornments and fur-trimmed long evening coats and capes; gentlemen handsomely attired in black tie, white tie and tails, derbies and top hats. Photographers and reporters were everywhere, attempting to bring the thrill of the evening to those reading their newspapers at home the next day.

Through Lela's job as theatrical reviewer for the *Fort Worth Record* Ginger saw and met not only all of these performers but also the managers of most of the theaters on the Interstate chain. By age 14, she had taken her first step on the road to success—eventually by way of Oregon. A win in a 1925 statewide Charleston competition held in the ballroom of the Baker Hotel in Dallas led to a four-week engagement on the Interstate circuit, followed by a three-year tour around the country. The tour of one-night stands included a stop at the Hunt's Craterian Theatre in Medford, Oregon, on April 21, 1926. The following day a picture of teenaged Ginger Rogers in the Medford *Mail Tribune* was captioned: "Miss Rogers is a winsome little miss with captivating mannerisms and a pair of feet that make the most intricate dances seem easy." Her appearance that day would mark the beginning of a lifelong tie to the region—and the Craterian, which would be renamed the Craterian Ginger Rogers Theatre in her honor years later.

When it had become apparent that Ginger's plans to become an English teacher would be tossed aside for a theatrical career, Lela eagerly pitched in to foster her daughter's dream by using her own skills, from making dresses, writing her material, coaching and chaperoning on tours, to overseeing contract negotiations, dressing room arrangements and finances. Along the way Lela Rogers established a reputation as a force to be reckoned with by driving hard bargains on her daughter's behalf.

Lela established such a stellar reputation that she was hired as an assistant to Charles Kerner, vice president in charge of production at RKO Pictures. She had been running an East Hollywood workshop called the Hollytown Theatre, where aspiring young actors trained and appeared in plays. Recognizing the value of her guidance, RKO execs asked Lela to shift her workshop activities to the Hollywood Playhouse, which was the small theater on the RKO lot. From 1938 to 1945 Lela ran the RKO Studios Workshop, developing new talent. Lela gave lessons to many of the young RKO contract players, including Betty Grable, Joy Hodges, Leon Ames, Anne Shirley, Phyllis Fraser and Tyrone Power. Of all of the aspiring actors in Lela's workshop, however, Maxine best remembers Lucille Ball. Then merely a RKO contract player, Lucille was appearing in an uncredited role as a fashion model in *Roberta*, starring Fred Astaire and Ginger Rogers, when she first met Lela Rogers. Lucille Ball would go on to buy the studio after she became a successful television star of the 1950s-'60s:

> Ginger's mother had a knack. She had an eye for talent; she just had a natural feeling for it. Once she saw what she could do for Ginger, she realized it—and it gave her the confidence she needed to know that she could spot talent. Then she started working at the [RKO] Studio, helping to develop some of the talent there. She loved what she did and realized she had this ability—and it paid very well.
>
> When Lucille Ball came along, Lela said, "By golly, what potential!" She told Lucille, "You've got a fabulous talent—and a good future ahead of you." It's a wonderful story.
>
> Lucille Ball came to her. Lela was sort of auditioning some people for her workshop and Lucille Ball was one of those who went to her—and she proved to be very good in some short plays and things Lela used to test their abilities.
>
> One day Lela talked to Lucille and said: "I've heard you're going with a gangster, or some guy." I don't remember his name or who he was. "If that's the truth, I cannot use you. But if you leave him *completely*, you show up tomorrow morning. If you don't feel that you want to leave him, don't come back."
>
> Lucille was there the next morning.
>
> Lela helped her develop her talent and brought her to the attention of movie executives. Lela worked with her ability as an actress. She saw potential that was dynamite, which is why she had said, "It's all or nothing." She was *so* helpful to her.
>
> That's the real story.

Ginger Rogers, Lucille Ball and Harriet Hilliard on the set of *Follow the Fleet*

Lucille Ball landed another role in Astaire and Rogers' second film, *Follow the Fleet*. By then, Lela Rogers had taken a special interest in developing Lucille's talent, which Lela recognized ahead of anyone else in Hollywood. In a 1992 interview with Leonard Maltin, Ginger Rogers elaborated on how her mother influenced Lucille Ball:

> My mother was very anxious for Lucille to be a star.
> She [mother] had a school there [RKO]. She taught acting to the kids who were assigned a small part, bit players. So she wanted them to do plays, where the various producers would come and see the plays, and say, 'I'd like that kid in my film." That's where Lucy started—and she was *good*, too. She was awfully good in plays. My mother said she was a *tyrant*. She was hard to manage because she always wanted to do it another way. Mother said, "No, you got to learn to be *obedient*." I'm glad she taught me that.

By 1933, Ginger Rogers and Fred Astaire were lighting up the silver screen as the dance team that would become the most acclaimed in American film history. It was only Astaire's second film appearance; for Ginger, it was her 20th. Despite her experience and acclaimed reputation, they would be billed

Ginger Rogers and Fred Astaire in *Swing Time*

as Fred and Ginger. When asked about her name following Astaire's, she said about the Hollywood industry: "It's a man's world." They had only supporting roles in their first outing together, *Flying Down to Rio*, but they had co-star billing in their next endeavor, *The Gay Divorcee* (1934). While they were providing uplift to a downtrodden nation, their brilliance also was inspiring a young dancer named Maxine Boura, who watched their every move over and over from her seat at Radio City Music Hall—*Flying Down to Rio, The Gay Divorcee, Roberta, Top Hat*. Although they would talk about their careers years later, Maxine said Ginger rarely spoke about dancing with Fred Astaire:

> I think Ginger said that her favorite film with Fred Astaire was *Swing Time*. I know she *loved* that film. But she also told me, "I love them all."
>
> Ginger said the same things as I did about dancing with Fred. She said he was wonderful, but "Oh, my!" The "oh, my" referred to his professionalism, of course, his obsession with perfection; but, she added, "That's what made us as good as we were."
>
> He was so precise about everything. Ginger said, "I had to give it my very best—everything I had in me, just to keep up with him."
>
> I knew exactly what she was talking about. He was *such* a perfectionist and carried it to more of an extreme than *anybody*

I've ever worked with in my life. But more than anything else, to me, was that he was so hard on himself—not giving himself any leeway.

She loved the feeling of independence when she and Fred finished their films together. She loved *Roxy Hart* (1942); she talked about it a lot. She loved doing films after she went out on her own.

By age 25, Ginger Rogers was an hugely successful movie star. When her marriage to Lew Ayres ended in May 1936, she moved into an apartment on Gregory Way with Lela. Ginger asked her mother if she would like it if she built a house for her and could live there with her. Lela consented and picked out a two-plus acre lot at 1605 Gilcrest Drive in Beverly Hills with a view of Catalina Island. The house plans included all of Ginger's desired amenities: a three-car garage, a swimming pool, the only en-tout-cas (fast-dry, crushed brick

Postcard shows one of Ginger Rogers' homes in Beverly Hills.

blended mixture) tennis court in Beverly Hills, an art studio that doubled as a guest cottage, a home theater and a soda fountain. It was there that Maxine first met the woman whom Ginger described in her autobiography as "the one [gift] I treasure above all others—my dear mother, Lela." Maxine remembers her early visits to the Beverly Hills home:

> I met Lela when I got out to California. She was living with Ginger. They had a home together in Beverly Hills. I spent a lot of time in that house, so I got to see her quite a bit.
>
> They lived on the top of a mountain with a tennis court and a swimming pool. The house itself was on something like a "hanger." It swung in a big hole. If there was an earthquake, the house would move, swing back and forth so the walls wouldn't crack or be damaged by the earthquake.
>
> They would have parties for Don and me or for her birthday or her mother's birthday. Ginger always had parties. She *loved* parties. She was very easy, very gentle with people. For instance, when people would recognize her out in public,

she was always so gracious and kind. She wasn't one of those who'd say, "Oh, I'm sorry. I can't bother with you today," or "I'm in a hurry"—those who'd make an excuse; and believe me, I've seen that *a lot*. Ginger would turn right around to the person who'd recognized her, and say, "Oh, aren't you nice to think of me." She was very, very humble and very sweet.

Clark Gable was the same way. No ego there. He used to say, "I have hands and a face. I can hear. I have a nose and a mouth like everybody else." And I would say to him, "yes, but it's *not* like everybody else!"

I will not tolerate phonies—and you meet so many phonies in this business. I don't go for that at all. I guess I was closest to people who were genuine; we'd have the same desire to be with somebody who's for real.

Although Maxine was raised Roman Catholic, her mother never had her baptized as she wanted Maxine to have the freedom to explore and be open to all religions. Non-practicing when her daughter was born, Lela Rogers turned to a Christian Scientist practitioner after Ginger was abducted by Lela's estranged husband and taken to Texas. The Christian Science faith continued to sustain her, as it would Ginger, who was a devoted Christian Scientist throughout her life. In following the tenets of her faith, Ginger did not smoke or drink, but there were some exceptions, says Maxine:

When we would go out, Ginger would always say, "Let me take a sip of your drink." She wouldn't drink, but she'd take a sip of my martini or whatever I was having. She didn't drink and she didn't smoke and she tried to keep as normal hours as she could. That work was pretty strenuous and she had sense enough to know that you couldn't burn the candle at both ends.

As with Maxine, Ginger possessed a deep sense of gratitude. Maxine's spiritual journey has always been an integral part of her life:

Thank God for your talent.

So many people in this business think it's they who have done it—and when they think they've done it by themselves, oh brother, you're going to have a tough time with that ego! They think they did it, not God. The ones who don't have gratitude are a pain in the butt!

Clark knew and Ginger knew and I knew that our talent was a gift from God. We were so lucky—and grateful.

Dancing with a Star

In the same way that Lela was instrumental in launching the careers of her daughter, Lucille Ball and others, Ginger, in turn, helped Maxine and Don when they went to Hollywood a couple years after they first met at New York's Copacabana. Ginger had love and a home designed for entertaining as well as an effervescent personality that drew people to her. Her numerous parties were well-attended events that found both friends and Hollywood A-listers gathered around her:

> *She* was the one who handled everything for us when we got out to California. Naturally we had called Ginger and told her that we were coming.
> She introduced us around to a lot of people, some directors, movie stars and some of her closet friends. She was *wonderful* from that standpoint. She tried to make everything easier for us because we were new out there and didn't know anybody. She had parties and we went out to dinner with people and so forth. It was wonderful. It helped us so much; I didn't feel so strange being out there.

It was most likely Ginger or Lela who first told Maxine about the experiments being conducted on the East Coast in something new called television. At a 1938 party in New York Lela had met a gentleman who was involved in this experimental field and was invited to his laboratory to see for herself what it was all about. The gentleman was most likely Allen B. DuMont, since it would have been easy to bring her to his laboratory located right across the Hudson River from Manhattan in Passaic, New Jersey. It is apparent that Lela and DuMont, who was proudly demonstrating his technological achievements in television, were far-sighted in looking to future possibilities of the new medium that would replace radio as the primary form of home entertainment.

Lela enthusiastically told Ginger what she had seen.

Maxine realized the days of the Barrat and Loper partnership would soon be over.

Immediately Lela thought of the implications for worldwide showings on television of Ginger's movies. Ginger's agent Leland Hayward brushed her off, however, and never had a clause providing for residuals added to her contract. As a result, neither Ginger nor Astaire—who had the same agent—ever received a dime for any subsequent showings of their films.

By the time Maxine met Lela in 1943, Maxine would have known that her time of dancing with Don Loper was running out. With her future uncertain, she would have listened very attentively to any talk about this new phenomenon of television. There might have been some speculative inducement for her to relocate to New York City for a job in the new medium or she might have conjured up some possibility in her own mind at that time. In either case, she was ready for any new opportunity that might emerge back in New York after the war.

Trade ad for *Thousands Cheer*, Don Loper and Maxine Barrat are in the bottom row on each end.

Once Maxine was settled into her new Hollywood lifestyle, she and Ginger spent as much time together as their hectic schedules would allow. They enjoyed shopping in some of the luxurious department stores of the day—Bullocks Wilshire, Robinson's, The Broadway-Hollywood—in spite of the risk of Ginger's being recognized out in public. Always meticulously dressed throughout her life, both personally and professionally, Maxine shared her fashion expertise with Ginger, who was grateful for the guidance:

> We used to go shopping together. That was a *gas!* When we weren't working or had some free time, she'd say, "C'mon, take me shopping!"
>
> And I'd say, "Okay."
>
> So, out we would go. But first she would have to put on a disguise of sorts because naturally everybody knew Ginger. She would wear dark glasses, and she would wear her hair under a small hat of some kind, not a very distinguished-looking one, but a nice hat to try to avoid being recognized.

And we'd get away with it for a while. But, it was so funny—because we'd go into these big department stores and start picking out things and chatting and everything—and all of a sudden, you'd see somebody stop and *stare*. They thought they knew who it was, but they weren't sure. Then somebody else would stop and stare. And they'd come over, and say, "Are you Ginger Rogers?" And Ginger would say to me, "Let's go!"

The magnificent, sometimes frivolous, costumes by top designers— Walter Plunkett, Edward Stevenson, Edith Head, Raoul Pène Du Bois, Madame Barbara Karinska and her personal favorites, Irene (Lentz) and Bernard Newman—created for Ginger Rogers to wow audiences in her 73 films are legendary. They ranged from enchanting, feminine dance gowns of ostrich feathers, beads, lace, chiffon, lamé, taffeta, satin to the publicity-rich mink and sequins, to pajamas, riding britches, boy shirts and the frilly ensembles in the fashion landmark film, *Top Hat*.

Perhaps the most famous of these magnificent creations was the original $30,000 faux ruby and emerald fur gown in *Lady in the Dark*. The gown was not used during

Ginger poses in her red-and-gold-sequined, mink-skirted gown designed for *Lady in the Dark*.

filming, however, as it was too heavy for Ginger to perform her routine, but it was later donated and displayed at the Smithsonian Institution. The total wardrobe cost for *Lady in the Dark* was a staggering $150,000 to $200,000. Ironically, in her personal life Ginger's choice of clothing did everything *but* wow crowds and she took a lot of good-natured teasing for some of her fashion faux pas, Maxine remembers:

The funny part about Ginger was that she did not have a flair for clothing.

Don said to her, "You're the worst-dressed person in California!" Don always said it like it was—and she loved him for it.

She said, "Okay, so design my clothes!" And he did! He designed a lot of clothes for her.

When she picked out her own clothes, she really didn't pick the best things for herself. It was remarkable that she had such wonderful taste in everything else but her clothes. She picked things that were not the most becoming.

When we'd go shopping, I'd try to guide her. She'd say to me, "Okay, Maxine, do you think this one's okay?"

I'd say, "Oh, Ginger, you can do better than that." Or, "That color isn't quite right for your skin."

I'd see her with a dress that really wasn't that becoming—and she could wear most anything, of course, but that wasn't the point. The point was to get something that was really lovely on her. There are women who just don't have a knack for choosing the right clothes for themselves. I was so surprised, of course, because Don and I were very fashion conscious—and, of course, I also designed clothes.

So, she'd say, "Look, I'll leave it to you."

Don let her know in no uncertain terms—most people wouldn't tell her, but he came right out with it. He'd say, "You look *lousy* in that color!"

Many times when we'd go shopping, we would get ahold of a salesperson and we would go into a dressing room instead of going out on the floor. If we went out on the floor, the first thing you know, you've got a crowd gathering around you. One person recognizes you and then everybody starts to talk. So what we do is have Ginger sit in a dressing room and I

Ginger Rogers had many talents, but fashion was not one of them.

Ginger Rogers

Tuesday the 13th

Darling,

Wondered where those dresses had originated. Think they are most attractive and am delighted that you thought to include me in your shopping. Size 10 fits me just wonderfully. Am considerably thinner than when you last saw me in New York (worry, worry, worry!) The material of the taffeta is exceptionally good...was surprised that it could be such lovely quality in so inexpensive a dress. These are certainly going to come in handy, dear, and please thank the firm of Filcol for wanting to send these things to me. I will be very happy to receive anything else that you may think suitable and will immediately return any that are not to my taste. You are really a doll-baby to do this for moi.

You might be interested to know that one of the pink hats you gave me before my departure, the heavy pink woven straw, I made into a very delightful summer hat and have worn it many times, each time thinking how very loving of you it was to snag these and give them to me.

Guess you have read my latest publicity, and perhaps you were already aware of this approaching thundercloud. It is too bad things have to end this way, but many times there is a blessing in it for all concerned.

Hope all is well with you. Have you seen Judi lately. She is a real elegant girl.

Much love to you and again, many, many thanks.

Lovingly,

Ginger

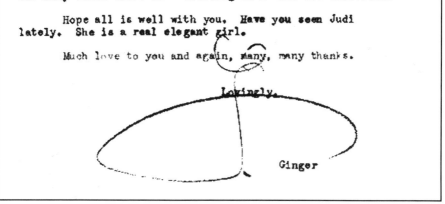

Letter to Maxine from Ginger Rogers

would go out with the salesgirl; we would pick out clothes for Ginger to start trying on—that way she wasn't out and around on the floor.

She was so grateful. She needed somebody to help her, and she *knew* it.

She would say, "Everybody tells me I look horrible—and Don makes me so aware of it! I'm afraid to pick out anything."

Some women would say, "I don't care what anybody thinks." But Ginger didn't have that attitude at all. She said, "I want to look my very best." So we tried to help her. She was so beautiful; she could wear anything, but there were some clothes that were just not very becoming.

Ginger Rogers and Don Loper in *Lady in the Dark*

Although Don Loper designed the costumes and did the staging for the reopening of New York's Copacabana in fall 1942, he and Maxine did not perform in the show due to a scheduling conflict.

In August, he had signed a contract to dance with Ginger Rogers in the film version of *Lady in the Dark,* which went into production in December; meanwhile Maxine was lined up for screen tests in anticipation of dancing with Fred Astaire in a Columbia Pictures production.

Don Loper may have first met and befriended Ginger Rogers when she appeared on Broadway in *Top Speed* (1929-30). At the time, Loper had been trying to break into theater, but his uncle had thwarted his efforts—and an opportunity to dance with her. Nonetheless, Loper leaped at an offer by Hollywood moguls years later to appear in Ginger's first color film, *Lady in the Dark*. Ginger's overtly demonstrative greeting of Loper upon his arrival in Hollywood prompted gossip of a new romance. They laughed it off, however, as Ginger was in a love-struck relationship with serviceman and part-time actor Jack Briggs, whom she would marry in January 1943; and, although Don Loper had been married three times (his last divorce was 1938), he preferred the company of men.

Dancing with a Star

Loper & Barrat were performing at the Copa when *Lady in the Dark*, starring Gertrude Lawrence as Liza Elliott, ran on Broadway (January 23, 1941 to May 30, 1942). For the subsequent ultra-lavishly produced RKO Pictures film adaptation of the hit musical, Ginger was cast in the role of Liza. In 1941, Ginger Rogers was Hollywood's highest paid female star and at the height of her career. Loper had the part of Adams, who would dance with Ginger in a surrealistic dream sequence amid a simulated fog created

Maxine takes a final bow with partner Don Loper and Copa production show members.

by dry ice. Although the film was shelved for a year and not released until 1944, critics would then cite their romantic routine performed to "Suddenly It's Spring" as one of the highlights of the film. As with Fred Astaire, Ginger spoke sparingly to Maxine about dancing with Don Loper:

> She danced with Don in *Lady in the Dark*, but she never said much about the film or dancing with him.
> It was a very beautiful number, but it was only one scene. Ginger loved dancing with him. She loved the way he moved. They danced beautifully together. No question about it. It was the only film they did together.

Watching films was a frequent, favorite pastime for Maxine and Ginger when they were together at her Beverly Hills home or the 4-R. They often rose early on the ranch, but not always:

> Ginger was unpredictable. Some days she just got lazy, especially if we were up the night before—and many times we were. We'd get caught up seeing some of her old films or seeing some films that she liked.
> She had a movie studio in her home in Beverly Hills downstairs. They would pull down a screen and show films, especially rushes [unedited film takes, usually prepared daily].

Ginger and Teresa Wright fish in one of the streams on Rogers' 4-R ranch.

When you had shot a film that day, they'd call that a rush—if you wanted to see it, to see how it looked and to decide if you should change it that day or the next day. Maybe it wasn't the right angle or maybe you didn't say your line as well as you would have liked to have said it, you'd say, "Let's re-do that scene."

So Ginger had this studio in the basement of her home—the room had been turned into a big beautiful room for viewing films. Very often she would show the rushes, what she'd filmed that day. They caught a lot of things that way.

When Maxine was under contract to dance with Fred Astaire, her experience with him was similar to Ginger's:

I did that, too, with Fred Astaire, when we were doing our film. We'd play the rushes, and say, "Gee, that could have been a better angle for doing that particular combination."

That was where you'd catch things early in the game so to speak.

They all had viewing rooms. That was a natural because they had to watch what they were doing every day.

Many times we'd review at the studio because we would have just finished, and we'd say, "Let's play it back." We would do that mostly with Fred.

But with Ginger it was mostly at her home.

After *The Story of Vernon and Irene Castle* wrapped (the ninth Astaire and Rogers film) they would only make one more film together. Ginger bought the 4-R, about 20 miles north of Medford. She would return to her beloved ranch many months each year for the next five decades to find solitude and escape from the Hollywood madness. "I consider myself an Oregonian," she once said. "I vote in Oregon and pay my taxes here." After Ginger sold the 4-R in 1992, she bought a house in Medford. Through the years, the Craterian, where she first had danced at age 15, remained a part of Ginger's life—and Maxine's visits:

Ginger Rogers poses on the tennis court.

If it were going to be a beautiful day, Ginger would say, "Let's go for a ride tomorrow." So we'd get up early, get dressed and go for a horseback ride on trails through the property. We'd do that early in the morning, if it weren't too hot. Or we'd go for a swim lots of times. We went fishing, too. It was just for fun. Mostly we caught little fish, but we'd throw them back. We'd take out the hook and give the little fish a pat on the back and say, "Now, you go swim home!"

She had a pool and a tennis court, of course. Ginger was a good tennis player; she was very good. She was passionate about it. We played. She was better than me though. I didn't get a chance to practice too much, but I loved it. I had a natural instinct for it. When you're a dancer, you have a natural instinct for some of these things. I was pretty good, but I couldn't compare with Ginger.

We'd always go back to the house for lunch, always, because they had help. Ginger had a thing about food. She loved vegetables. Good food. The cook at the ranch was excellent. We'd have lunch and sometimes Ginger would take a nap in the afternoon. She would say, "I don't do this often, but when I need it, I need it!" So after lunch she might go and rest for a while.

Many times we'd have people in for dinner or we'd go to somebody's home for dinner. Or we'd go to the theater. If there were a show that we wanted to see, we would drive into town [Medford] and see it. We'd stay overnight, and the next morning we'd drive back out to the ranch.

farthest distance of all 60 guests, who had come from all over the country to celebrate with Ginger that evening:

> Judi had worked for Ginger at one time. She had been a chorus girl, maybe at Metro. She was lovely, so pretty, red hair and a beautiful figure. She had worked as a secretary for Ginger in California, so she had that connection.

For quite some time, Ginger had resided in Rancho Mirage, her final winter home and safe haven—along with her church. She spent her summers in Medford, Oregon, where she continued to support and give presentations at the Craterian Theatre. On Sunday afternoon, November 21, 1993, nearly seven decades after she first appeared at the Craterian, Ginger returned to its stage. A capacity crowd listened attentively as newsman Al Reiss interviewed the "Queen of the Silver Screen;" a Q&A session followed. The event concluded with the showing of *Roxie Hart*, "one of my favorite films," said Ginger.

Mrs. Lela Rogers passed away on May 25, 1977, at the age of 85. Ginger Rogers died at her Rancho Mirage home on April 25, 1995. She was 83. Sadly, Maxine did not attend her dear friend's funeral:

Ginger Rogers

I did not *know* about it. Something kept me from going—I think
I was in Europe. I didn't even hear about it until I got back.

Ginger Rogers was cremated and her ashes were interred next to her
mother's—only a few yards away from Fred Astaire's grave—at Oakwood
Memorial Park Cemetery in Chatsworth, California.

Chapter Eleven
New York to New Orleans—and Back

In the days before a/c was common, Monte Proser closed down the Copacabana for the hot summer months and shifted the entire staff to the Piping Rock, a Moorish-style gambling establishment on the outskirts of Saratoga Springs, New York. The picturesque upstate sulfur-spring spa town, with its huge elm tree-lined Grand Avenue boasting two of the largest hotels in the world, was a prime resort for organized crime, politicians and high society during the August horseracing and social season. Nightlife revolved around the luxurious casinos, or "carpet joints," the most famous of which were the Brook Club, Meadowbrook and Piping Rock. Loper and Barrat were among the acts hired in 1941 to perform in Monte Proser's no-expense-spared Copacabana Revue at the Piping Rock.

Mob kingpin Meyer Lansky used the cover of the existing restaurant at the Piping Rock to conceal an illegal gambling casino operation—in an adjacent building—which was guarded from local authorities. Lansky had brought in as part owner Mafia Godfather-Copa boss Frank Costello, who utilized the resources of his (mob-controlled but Proser operated) New York Copacabana nightclub to provide fine cuisine, service and entertainment for the swanky Piping Rock supper club. A new show was put together with fresh material, including production numbers, costumes and a line of Samba Sirens comprised of girls who were free for the summer season. The Piping Rock told a story of opulence, elegance and wealth, intriguing the imaginations of those not among its privileged clientele:

Postcard featuring Piping Rock

It was *so beautiful*. The casinos, of course, made it so fabulous.

There were people from New York [City], people on vacation—all glamorous, all wealthy people ready to spend their money. There was money, money, money everywhere.

After the folding of the Saratoga summer tent, Loper and Barrat went right into rehearsal for the much anticipated Copacabana reopening, which in time would become an annual highlight of the fall entertainment season in New York. A new personality named Aurora, younger sister of the famous Carmen Miranda, along with a colorful, lively cariocan revue, was scheduled for the

MAN ABOUT MANHATTAN

By GEORGE TUCKER

NEW YORK—You like Carmen Miranda, who sings about the "Souse" American Way?

That's too bad, because this isn't about Carmen—it's about her sister, Aurora, a sloe-eyed gal from Brazil who hopes to make her own way without leaning too heavily on her sister's current red-hot vogue.

Aurora never worked in an American nightclub until she opened as the high priestess of the new revue at the Copacabana a few nights ago. But she has had plenty of cabaret experience at home. She is the girl about whom the song was written, the one named "Aurora." She's 22.

Though her gowns are tropics-inspired, she shies away from the "bahiana" headdress popularized by her sister. This is the head-dress inspired by a basket of fruit. The name comes from Bahia. Brazil's fourth largest city. A girl who comes from Bahia is known as a Bahiana. Aurora and Carmen and their sister, the latter now retired to domesticity, are all Bahianas.

* * *

IT is Aurora's ambition to give "Norse" America a little of the "Souse" American comedy in the form of songs. But you will have to be Portuguese to understand what they are about. One number her animated antics and facial highjinks have built into a stopper is called "Arca de Noe," which means Noah's Ark. The weird noises drifting to my ear as she sang suggested the Latinized cries and chatter of the beasts as they boarded the arc. Another number, "Kangeru," is about Kangaroos, and Aurora has to hop like one.

She's a striking looking gal with clothes that cling and seem to have been suggested by the corals, yellows and greens of the jungle foliage.

When she came to this country her agents wanted to bill her as Aurora Miranda, but Aurora put a stop to that fast. "In this country Miranda means Carmen—I'm Aurora."

* * *

YOU will admit that the Northern Lights make a strange name for a girl born in Brazil. It happened this way: Aurora was born about 6 o'clock one morning. Her father, slightly jittery at the moment, was pacing the floor. At 6 a.m. the old Doc shoved his head through the door and said something like this: ."Hey, it'sa fine. She'sa girl."

Papa fetched a jubilant sigh. He glanced out the window. The sun was just breaking across the yard. "We'll call her Aurora," he decided.

That's what the New Yorkers are calling her, too. They call for more and more. The night I was there they called her for six encores.

reopening.

Monte Proser's method of publicizing Aurora's upcoming appearance and capitalizing on Loper and Barrat's recent travels and innovative choreography was typical of his inventive press agentry. Aurora, who used only her first name professionally, was linked with the previous year's Rio carnival hit, "Aurora," which was used as the Copa's finale number in the last show before its summer closing. Now Proser was publicizing his headliner Aurora as the inspiration for importing the Brazilian song to America. Proser's other nod to Latin American goodwill was Loper and Barrat, newly returned from the Southern Hemisphere. There was much excitement and preparation for their performance of "Tico Tico," which was to be presented for the first time in the United States with orchestral arrangement by Frank Marti, maestro of the Copa's samba band.

The thrill and electricity of the filled-to-capacity opening night, October 2, 1941, was captured by the *New York Sun*'s Malcolm Johnson:

> Judged by nightclub standards, or from the viewpoint of owners who, quite understandably, like to see a packed house, the reopening of Monte Proser's Copacabana on Thursday night was a brilliant success.
>
> Everybody was there—everybody! The management packed the paying customers in layers. And they do say that loads of people, including important people, waited patiently in the foyer for what would pass as a table.

The dressed-up, classy Copa clientele included big-name stars and other celebrities of the day. Hollywood star Randolph Scott could be seen seated at a dime-sized table with New York Yankees owner Dan Topping and ice skating Olympic gold medalist Sonja Henie. Actor George Raft was there, as were the Ritz Brothers, slapstick comedy trio—stars of stage, screen and later television. Also present in honor of her sister's opening night was Carmen Miranda, along with a Brazilian entourage.

Variety lavished praise on Loper and Barrat:

Dancing with a Star

Monte Proser's Copacabana has reopened with a new personality, Aurora, sister of Carmen Miranda, heading the gay, cariocan revue which is replete with a wealth of beauty and talent. Not the least of this are Loper and Barrat, with their finished dancing, doing an unusual American dance routine to the *Bandwagon* [Broadway musical revue, 1931-32] score and encoring with "Tico Tico no Fubá," in keeping with the Latin legit motif of the revue.

Loper and Barrat were a windfall for Monte Proser. The dance team was directly responsible not only for resurrecting the Copacabana floorshows but also for making the samba the nightly highlight of the current review. They successfully reignited a late 1930s abortive attempt to popularize the samba and almost single-handedly established it as the latest dance rage. Little could Monte Proser have foreseen that, when he took a gamble and tried them out in the spring show, one of the payoffs would be the Copa's getting credit for the soaring popularity of the samba. In many respects Loper and Barrat were as much responsible for establishing the club's world-famous reputation as the Great American Nightclub as the Copa was for being a ticket to ports of call around the world.

Proser wanted to use the allure of Loper and Barrat in conjunction with bringing in a big-name act to offset production show competition from other nightclubs. By inaugurating a name show policy, Proser hoped to move the Copa beyond its strictly authentic South American offerings to become the New York headquarters for great stars. The combined South American flavor and star quality of Loper and Barrat would provide Monte Proser with a perfect bridge for a transition in production styling. Maxine's appealing beauty was another draw not lost on Monte Proser, as underscored by columnist George Tucker: "The fine success enjoyed by Loper & Barrat, dancers, goes straight back to the truism that two-thirds of the attractiveness of any dance team depends on how stunning the woman is."

For the Copa's first anniversary show Proser contracted musical comedy and radio star of the 1930s, Gertude Niesen, whose biggest success would come a few years later in *Follow the Girls* (1945) with a then-unknown comic named Jackie Gleason. Meanwhile, Proser had negotiated for Joe E. Lewis as the first stand-up comic to play the midnight show for three weeks, opening New Year's Eve 1941; Lewis already was booked to star in *The Lady Comes Across* at the 44th Street Theatre and was not available for all the Copa shows.

Loper and Barrat, who would be held over until the Copa closed in June and then be part of the summer revue at Piping Rock, rendered continuity to the floorshow layout and brought in the crowds. "My idea of a smooth, easy-to-watch dance team is the expert duo of Maxine Barrat and Don Loper," Dorothy Kilgallen penned in her November 25, 1941 column. A photograph of them taken while performing that fall season at the Copacabana with one of its trademark white palm trees in the background graced the cover of *The American Dancer*, December 1941. *Variety* praised:

> Don Loper and Maxine Barrat continue with their socko terps. Seemingly Miss Barrat has her dancing partner make her the same gowns in sundry colors, since she favors a like pattern, but in different shades. The couturier appurtenances are as distinctive as their terps, although something should be done by dance stager Billy Reed to permit Loper to mop his brow and give him respite.
>
> It's a grueling grind he goes through, first with the team's Youmans medley [replacing the former Arthur Schwartz *Bandwagon* music]; and then he does things with the Samba Sirens…Miss Barrat has an opportunity to catch her breath but not he.

With the bombing of Pearl Harbor on December 7, 1941 the lives of all Americans changed. In the months to come droves of men enlisted in the armed forces as women took to the work force and tended their victory gardens. Entertainment provided a respite from war weariness. Flashy, elaborate floorshows and paradoxical gaiety abounded in nightclubs, which thrived despite our country's involvement in World War II. "The pace was not sweet, but hot," remarked *Variety*'s Abel Green. Copa operators considered merely fair a weekly revenue of $45,000, while a Joe E. Lewis-Loper and Barrat billing brought in over $50,000 a week.

A port of embarkation for Europe, New York played host to military personnel on the move. Entertainment venues like the Copacabana quickly established a reputation for hospitality to members of the armed services. Copa stars as well as the Samba Sirens contributed to the war effort in various ways. For their part, Loper and Barrat would be named co-chairmen of the February 1942 nightclub unit of the American Theatre Wing funddrive-cocktail party at the Copa to raise funds to supply canteens for army camps. They also entertained servicemen on leave at the American Theatre Wing's 44th Street Stage Door Canteen; Dorothy Kilgallen gave them a special mention in her column for teaching the samba to 50 soldiers and sailors at the recreational center.

The Copa's Samba Sirens

The Joe E. Lewis–Loper and Barrat pairing rang in the new year, 1942, with a landslide business that made the cash registers ching—much to the delight of Copa management. Lewis' three-week contract was renegotiated and he was held over. Lewis and Loper and Barrat would perform three shows nightly for an unprecedented number of weeks into the fall of 1942 that included a five-week summer stint at Copa-affiliated Piping Rock. The fast pace was exhilarating, but exhausting:

Soldiers welcome in the New Year of 1942 at the New York Copa.

It was an amazing life. We finished the last show at the Copa and got out by 3:30 in the morning. We would have breakfast at 4 a.m. and go to bed about 6. We were on that tight schedule: three shows a night and sometimes other performances in between.

Nightclub entertainers, like dancers and singers, need special costuming for their acts but find it difficult to shop regular store hours. As entertainers we work 'til early hours of the morning and our daily routines take place at hours most people don't see because they are asleep. Performers' sleep can take place at any hour, even between shows, but shopping must be done when the stores are open to the public. Most showbiz people sleep their eight hours from 4 a.m. to noon; at noon begins a schedule of physical exercise, practice and rehearsals, quick meals and wardrobe preparation. Make-up, hair and wardrobe are paramount to the pizzazz of acts booked at major venues. Costume fittings and shopping for clothes must be accomplished during morning store hours so as not to take time from afternoon rehearsals, practice and auditions.

One time, Don had to pick up spats to complete a stage outfit for another show. We did not sleep our normal eight hours because we had to be at Macy's when the doors opened at 10 a.m. in order to get to rehearsal later that morning.

Don's request for spats sent a store clerk on a quest to find them. She observed that we were two very tired-looking customers; she assured us she'd return promptly. Despite her promise, the clerk did not return promptly—at least not soon enough for Don and me to remain standing while waiting. We—the glamorous nightclub entertainers who were so fatigued—

waited and waited. Finally giving in to our exhaustion and tired feet, we sat down on a furniture display. When the clerk returned with the spats, she found us seated in the middle of a bustling sales floor, clunked together on a couch beneath an "On Sale" sign.

We were leaning on each other, shoulder to shoulder, head to head, sound asleep in the middle of Macy's department store! Can you imagine? We had gone to bed at 6 a.m. and were at Macy's when they opened at 9 or 10. I don't know how we did it, but you just do.

Along with garnering rave reviews with dance partner Maxine Barrat, multi-talented Don Loper was becoming more involved in other aspects of the show. With the opening of the February 5, 1942 Copa show he was selecting the Samba Sirens, staging the show and appearing with Maxine Barrat as one of its stars. While he always had designed Maxine's ensemble from head to toe, Loper now was designing every garment and headpiece worn in the entire production. Whereas the Samba Sirens originally had been dressed individually, now the line of girls was presented in the same exquisite costuming, a trend that changed very little over the ensuing years. Many of the elements of Maxine's attire that were becoming hallmarks of Loper's style—long gloves and hair adornments or hats were used to create a new look for the Samba Sirens. *Billboard* praised:

Don Loper designed all of Maxine's dance costumes.

Don Loper and Maxine Barrat, who have become big favorites here, punched across a fast foxtrot, then a waltz medley and then a samba to "Tico Tico No Fubá." Miss Barrat's costume is a draped affair that reveals her slender legs in tantalizing fashion. Loper, who designs his partner's unusual gowns, will design the costumes for the Copa's new February 4 show, *Flying Down to Rio.* This will be the first time Miles White will not be doing the Copa costumes.

Flying Down to Rio was the title of the 1933 RKO film and first outing for Fred Astaire and Ginger Rogers, who did "The Carioca" and set a precedent for films to come. The Copa's *Flying Down to Rio-and Back* was a two-part extravaganza depicting a journey to the Southern Hemisphere at the 8 p.m. dinner show and returning north of the equator at suppertime (midnight), with highlights of both presented at the 2:00 a.m. performance. The production was a lively, colorful fashion showcase for Loper, whose genius for costume design made his talents the highlight of this lavish production. Critics rated this show as one of the best to date. Abel Green reported:

> Evidently catching Monte Proser on an offbeat, Loper got permission to shoot the works. Plus his own good taste and originality, very evident in some $14,000 that was spent in executing Loper's designs into silks and stuff. That the getups drew applause at each new appearance opening night was voluble praise for the dancer's excellent job.
>
> Besides the designing, the male half of the fine Loper and Barrat dance team did a good job staging the Copa's new show, and the team continues as an important part of the nitery's entertainment itself.

... G-Man Hoover's hobby is cowboy films ... Most costly patriotic note is the red, white and blue necklace Maxine (Copa) Barrat wears. Paul Flato made it for her to model. Value is 50 Gs ... Iris Marshall, showgal at La Mar-

Walter Wincehll column April 5, 1942

In a February 22, 1942 *New York Times* article, "Scored for the Dance," six dancers of Broadway fame were pictured in designer creations, with shorter, "modern five-to-dawn" skirt lengths for dress-up occasions. Maxine was featured wearing a Loper-designed tailored suit that started a new trend in nightclub attire. Loper also became known for some of his novelty creations, including gloves worn by Maxine that were trimmed in phosphorescent strips that glowed in the dark.

Maxine's high profile made her popular among designers who wanted to capitalize on the press accorded her. At one time more popular than Tiffany and Co. or Harry Winston, star-socialite-heir jewelry designer Paul Flato created a red, white and blue necklace for Maxine to model that was valued at $50,000. Maxine wore hundreds of thousands of dollars worth of jewelry while performing on the Copa dance floor, where four uniformed and armed guards often kept a watchful eye from its four corners:

> It belonged to Winston Jewelers. They sold millions of dollars worth right off my back.

Dancing with a Star

One night a man bought a $100,000 necklace I was wearing. It made the picture page of the *New York Daily News*.

Loper and Barrat were a mainstay of the Copacabana shows from fall 1941 to June 1942. The Copa management wanted to assure the public that the beloved dance team would continue to be held over by including the following tagline in print ads, "...*and of course* Don Loper & Maxine Barrat." Concurrently with performing in the Copa shows, Loper and Barrat participated at special events under the auspices of the Copacabana as well as independently. In addition to co-chairing the nightclub unit of the American Theatre Wing fund drive-cocktail party at the Copa in early February, Loper and Barrat joined other entertainers, including comedian Phil Baker, actor-comedian Jerry Lester, flamenco dancers Antonio and Rosario and the Samba Sirens for the Treasurers' Club of America benefit held at the Waldorf-Astoria in April 1942. Maxine also was among such celebrities as Danny Kaye, Gertrude Lawrence, Sophie Tucker, Arlene Francis and Kay Kyser on March 22nd when they drew soldiers' names out of a hat—the lucky winners received gift packages from Gimbel's department store and their "Express Your Gratitude" campaign. In May, Loper and Barrat were among the entertainers for the Ziegfeld Club Ball benefit held on the Starlight Roof of the Waldorf-Astoria under the direction of Hassard Short, Eddie Cantor and emcee Jimmy Walker.

A feature article about Loper and Barrat titled "New York's Smoothest Dance Team" appeared in the June 2, 1942 issue of *Look*. The predominantly pictorial two-page spread illustrated how, "Style, grace and comedy fuse in Loper and Barrat routines." Loper and Barrat had become the most highly acclaimed ballroom dance duo since Vernon and Irene Castle, and comparisons frequently were drawn between them. "One of the newest dances is the 'Dengoza,' a type of dance popularized by the Castles and seldom attempted by anyone since the last war," declared George Tucker, for instance. "For this number Peter De Rose wrote the music, 'The American Waltz.' Loper insists it is prettier than even 'Deep Purple,' which De Rose wrote...."

Both teams exuded elegance and made dancing seem effortless, while the partners projected a delight in dancing with each other. As the Castles had led the craze for ragtime and theatrical routines as social dances before WWI,

Maxine Barrat patrolling her air raid warden beat in evening clothes and enough jewels to light a total blackout. . . . Allan Jones striding up 5th hatless — (and such shoulders!). ... Francis Lederer, who wears his hair over his eye, leading into the 1-2-3 a huge English sheepdog — with exactly the same coiffure! . . . The Jolly Rogerses—Buddy and his Mary Pickford — snatching a snack at Jack Dempsey's inn. . . . Bonnie Baker snoozing backstage at the Hurricane, just before the 2 a. m. show. . . . Loretta Young giving the Colony its oomph for the day.

Kilgallen

⌣ ⁕ ⌣

Loper and Barrat now were doing the same for the samba during WWII. Irene Castle had been a trendsetter with her bobbed hairdo, headache bands, bonnets, shoes and flowing frocks. Now Maxine was influencing fashion with her Loper-designed attire, considered among the most beautiful of the day. "Loper and Barrrat have been called successors to the Castles, pace-setting dancers of World War I days," *Look* proclaimed. "Maxine, like Irene Castle, is 'Best Dressed Dancer' of her time."

When the Copa shuttered for the summer, the show traveled to New Orleans intact, except for Carol Bruce, where it opened on June 4, 1942 at the elegant Blue Room in the Hotel Roosevelt. The Blue Room, dubbed "the town's swankiest nitery," was considered one of the country's premier venues for nationally touring musical acts at the height of the supper club era.

Headliners Loper and Barrat topped a lively south-of-the-border revue that received rave reviews for its wealth of beauty and talent, which included Juanita Alvarez, a vocalist reminiscent of Carmen Miranda who sang in her native tongue; dancers Walter Long and Betty Jane Smith; long-time Copa tenor-dancer Fernando Alvares; and six Samba Sirens, including Lucille Bremer, who would go on to Hollywood acting-dancing fame. New to the Roosevelt was the Boyd Raeburn Orchestra, which played for the production numbers and dancing. Shortly after its opening, *Variety* forecast that the lively revue showed every indication of becomming the biggest draw the city's top venue had ever had—due in large measure to headliners Loper and Barrat: "Topping the entertainers are Don Loper and Maxine Barrat, a classy ballroom team performing unusual routines which drew plenty of palm-pounding from first nighters. Style is smooth, easy and eyepleasing, offering some slick variations of the usual ballroom terps."

Unlike her smooth, easy dance performances, Maxine's personal life was awhirl. She found herself caught up in a steamy romance that tipped her completely off balance—and ended in marriage. *Variety* announced:

WED: Maxine Barrat to Jerry Haskell, in St. Bernard, La., June 27. Bride is half of Loper and Barrat ballroom dance team; groom is N.Y. advertising man.

Dancing with a Star

In her June 25, 1942 column Dorothy Kilgallen wrote: "Maxine Barrat's elopement in New Orleans with NY ad executive Jerry Haskell was the fastest boy-meets-girl blisskrieg of the season. They met on Saturday, were married on Sunday!"

Maxine first met Haskell at a party given by him for the purpose of meeting her. When she departed New York for New Orleans, he followed her. Maxine explains what happened:

That marriage was short-lived. It was just too much "happy stuff!"

I remember saying to him, "This is insane because I have a career with Don. I don't have any time to be married." And that's how we got un-did!

After we got married, I knew it was a mistake. I said, "This is bad for you because I'm traveling all the time." I had forgone that once before to marry somebody else [Joe Levine]—one of my young sweethearts. I had said the same thing to him, "Look, I'm going to have a career. I'll never be here. I won't be like a wife who you can travel with, be with—I'll be traveling with Don. I'll be away. What kind of a wife would that be?"

The way we had met was, he gave a big party and invited people I knew because he wanted to meet me. He invited the man I was going with at the time and he brought me to the party. The point was, he gave the party so that he could meet me.

He [Haskell] followed me to New Orleans, and he gave me this whirlwind of a ride. And I mean a *whirlwind!* I was extremely overwhelmed.

Then I thought, "What have I done? I can't fulfill the obligations of marriage." So I said to him, "This is crazy. We have to get it annulled."

> the practice. . . . Jerry Haskell, who a couple of seasons ago was married to and separated from Maxine Barrat in less than 24 hours, is now pursuing Nancy Callahan, the showgirl. . . . Raymond

Maxine's marriage to Jerry Haskell was annulled the following year. By then, she was involved in a serious romance with Rita Hayworth's ex-husband Ed Judson. Her photograph with the title "Cuts 'Kissless' Tie" appeared in newspapers nationwide in mid-August 1943, with the caption:

> Pretty Maxine Barrat, New York dancer, told the judge that her one-hour marriage to producer-playboy Jerry Haskell was of the "kissless" variety. Her lawyer also pointed out that Haskell had been divorced before and needed court permission to remarry. The judge set Maxine free.

When the final curtain came down on the show at the Hotel Roosevelt, Loper and Barrat, Carol Dexter, Betty Jane Smith and Fernando Alvares packed their bags and traveled north to Saratoga Springs, where they were joined by Joe E. Lewis, Estelita, and six Samba Sirens for the summer revue at the Piping Rock. Paul

Baron's orchestra alternated with the Copa's own Frank Marti's samba band for musical accompaniment. The show was designed, costumed and directed by Don Loper, who also designed a pair of shoes for Maxine that attracted a lot of attention. "The Saratoga customers, who are used to practically anything, are nevertheless gasping these nights at the shoes—with ruby-encrusted heels!—that Don Loper designed for his partner, Maxine Barrat," Dorothy Kilgallen remarked.

While committed wholeheartedly to their dance partnership, Loper and Barrat also worked separately on occasion. For example, Monte Proser had

Maxine and Don Loper pose in the Blue Room in New Orleans.

hired Don Loper to costume and stage the Copacabana reopening show in Fall 1942, but he and Maxine did not perform in it as schedules conflicted; Loper had signed in August with RKO Pictures to dance with Ginger Rogers in the film version of *Lady in the Dark*, with filming to commence December 1942. Meanwhile it was announced in *Variety* that Maxine was slated for a screen test in anticipation of signing to dance with Fred Astaire in a forthcoming Columbia Pictures musical:

> Fred Astaire came to me and asked if I would like to do a film with him.
>
> "Would I like to?" I said, "Fred, I would *love* it. Of course I'd be so thrilled!"
>
> So we went into rehearsal. For the first few days I was so nervous trying to keep up with him. He realized it and he was so sweet.
>
> He'd say, "That's okay, Maxine, let's do it again."
>
> After several days—and this was quite an amazing thing for me—all of a sudden, Fred made a mistake. I was shocked

because what he did was go over to a hard wall and he hit his foot against that wall.

I said, "Fred, what are you doing? Are you crazy—those talented feet—how can you do that?"

He very calmly walked by me, and he said in the most disgusted voice, *"They're not supposed to make a mistake."* If that wasn't a shock! He was amazing. His attitude was so calm but he was *so* angry with himself.

I said, "But it's only a little mistake, Fred." He made such a big deal. To him, it was. Mister Perfectionist.

A few minutes later he was fine.

He was fabulous to work with and a couple of times we had it filmed in rehearsal clothes, just to see how it looked. Once we'd see it, he'd say, "Let's change the camera angle on this, or something." We had a few of those done. We had a couple of numbers all set and ready to go, and we were so happy.

All of a sudden, the powers-to-be came to us and said, "We've got to stop production."

"Why?"

They couldn't agree on the storyline and it would take two or three months to rewrite the whole thing. They just weren't getting anywhere. They tried, and they just weren't happy with the storyline.

So that's the one thing in my life that I did *not* finish that I was very sad about because I so enjoyed working with him.

In early October, Loper and Barrat were featured in a stage bill of four acts at the Loew's State Theatre, one of New York's grand, elaborately decorated movie palaces. The William Morris Agency decided to employ the same winning formula of having two of its top acts in the same show, billing both Loper and Barrat and Joe E. Lewis, who then was doubling at the Copa. "Miss Barrat wears one of the most sensational evening gowns this reviewer has seen…" praised *Billboard.* Presented in conjunction with the premier of *Somewhere I'll Find You* (M-G-M), the stage show also included singer (Wee) Bonnie Baker and the unicycling Four Sidneys. Dorothy Kilgallen commented on some of the Loper and Barrat admirers in the audience: "Samba Sirens attending Don Loper and Maxine Barrat's performance at Loew's State—the cutest upsweep-headed row in town!" *Variety* praised Loper and Barrat's contribution to the theater's impressive weekly box office of approximately $30,000:

Loper and Barrat on the marquee of Loew's State Theatre

Classy dance team is on just before Lewis; they are Don Loper and Maxine Barrat, both rating high in their field. Appearance of Miss Barrat certainly helps. Ballroom duo drew an excellent score, earning two encores.

With the State Theatre chore completed Loper and Barrat traveled back to New Orleans. They were booked for their second appearance at the Blue Room with emceeing Ted Weems and his orchestra, Latin songstress-Copa alum Rosita Rios and acrobatic dancer Margery Faye. Fronting the smoothly rhythmic Weems orchestra was featured vocalist Perry Como, who was still with the group but soon would go out on his own and become one of America's most popular crooners:

> This is when I originally met Perry [Como]. We instantly became friends. He was the sweetest guy in the whole world. He was one of the biggest stars, but you'd never know it; he was so unassuming.
>
> Five years later I walked into a room and he was there. "Maxine," he called out to me. As big a star as he was, he remembered me and came over to greet me.

Maxine Barrat and Don Loper's appearances were frequent topics for New York gossip columns.

Loper and Barrat received special mention among the floorshow's three acts in *Variety*'s review of the Saturday, October 24, 1942 show: "Topping the entertainment are Don Loper and Maxine Barrat, a classy ballroom team who are no strangers here. Their style is smooth, easy and eye-pleasing. Miss Barrat is attractive, and she and Loper kept the first nighters asking for more." The dance team that had been turned away by William Morris before scoring at a Copacabana debut in spring 1941 had become one of its stellar acts, an example of the agency's talent to nurture what it called "the stars of the future." As a William Morris Agency ad once proclaimed, "Our small act of today is our big act of tomorrow." For Maxine it meant living her wildest childhood dreams to become, in the words of one Broadway wag, "one of the dancing darlings of the early '40s."

The fame that Loper and Barrat were enjoying, however, had not spread beyond North and South America. That was about to change.

Chapter Twelve
From the City of Light to M-G-M Kleig Lights

The William Morris Agency had bold plans for Loper and Barrat. Even as the duo glided over the highly polished floorboards of the magnificent Blue Room at the Hotel Roosevelt, their next career move was being shaped a thousand miles away in the RKO Building offices 28 floors above Radio City Music Hall at Rockefeller Center. Transatlantic calls coming in to the bustling Morris offices from leading hotels and nightclubs abroad had prompted preparations for a Loper and Barrat European tour. It was time for the nationally acclaimed dance team to take the leap onto a broader international stage.

Before embarking on their overseas tour, the famed dance team was tapped to headline at the opening of the new Ciro's, the legendary celebrity hangout located at 8433 Sunset Boulevard on the Sunset Strip, playground of the stars. As Loper was already slated to be in California to dance with Ginger Rogers in *Lady in the Dark*, which was due to begin filming in December 1942, an engagement at Ciro's tied in perfectly for Loper and Barrat.

Opened in January 1940, the nightclub had fallen into a slump as did the other clubs on Sunset Boulevard by mid-1942, when Herman (H.D.) Hover took it over from Billy Wilkerson. Hover renovated the interior, installed theatrical dimmers, removed mirrors in the main room and added a ladies' lounge complete with a 20th Century-Fox studio-inspired, bulb-studded make-up mirror. Appealing to glitterati and proletariat alike, Hover instituted policies to recreate the same sense of camaraderie that had made the then-thriving Hollywood

Ciro's dance floor in 1942

Canteen so successful; he also abandoned Wilkerson's no-entertainment policy. Hover wanted a top-notch act to bring in the crowds for the new Ciro's opening night and hired Loper and Barrat as headliners to augment Al Donohue and his orchestra. A Christmas Eve 1942 ad in the *Reporter* promised "An Evening of Revelry." Opening night was a typically stellar Hollywood occasion with stars showing up in droves. Among the many movie stars present were Lana Turner, Cary Grant, Joan Crawford, Mickey Rooney, Jimmy Durante and an army-uniformed Desi Arnaz with his date, Lucille Ball. Ciro's reputation as a place to see and be seen in Hollywood would rival that of New York's Copacabana:

> Ginger came to see Don and me at Ciro's before we moved to California. She came with some of her friends when we first opened. There were about six of them at the table that night.

With memories of a fabulous stand at Ciro's fresh in their minds, Loper and Barrat set their sights on their 1943 overseas tour. Maxine said:

> After our success in Rio and the United States, we could pretty much write our own ticket. We danced all over the world in beautiful nightclubs and hotels. We even danced for the King of Denmark.

Although Denmark was under Nazi occupation at the time, most Danish institutions continued to function relatively normally with the government more or less intact. The Danish head of state remained at the grand palace and continued to entertain guests. As it happened, the Loper and Barrat royal engagement was not part of the itinerary crafted by William Morris but came about serendipitously:

> Apparently he had heard about us before we ever arrived there. He'd seen a newsreel clip or something.
> Evidently word got to the King that we were going to be in Europe. So he figured since we would be in Europe anyway, maybe we'd like to come and dance for him.
> He was going to give a party, so he asked if we would perform at the palace for it. So off we went to Denmark.

Dancing for King Christian X of Denmark in the magnificent rococo ballroom at the Royal Palace in Copenhagen turned out to be one of the highlights of their tour. Maxine wistfully recalls meeting and dancing for the Danish monarch and his guests:

I met him, of course; he was charming. He was married, but his wife was with her family or off on a trip somewhere or something; she wasn't there.

He made us feel very at ease, I must say. He was easy to talk to and very complimentary.

There was also a singer, a wonderful young female vocalist—and us.

Dancing at the palace was quite thrilling, quite lovely and very charming. It was a big ballroom—very large. It was a big audience. It was all the people he had surrounding him and his friends. It was quite a group; I'd say maybe a hundred people. It was such a thrill. Oh, the charm, the warmth and the beauty.

He took us around to see the castle. Beautiful paintings everywhere. All European furniture—which is so different from ours. Everything was so elegant. It was like being in a museum. It was absolutely magnificent.

From Denmark, Loper and Barrat traveled to England. Among the first stops of the London phase of their scheduled tour was the magnificent Dorchester Hotel. After the demolition in 1929 of the once palatial private residence known as Dorchester House, the Dorchester Hotel was opened on April 18, 1931. Located on Park Lane in the West End of London's exclusive Mayfair district in the city of Westminster, the hotel has commanding views of Hyde Park, one of the city's great parks. At the time the Dorchester was known for its magnificent 1,200-person capacity ballroom, where Loper and Barrat dazzled hotel patrons with their

King Christian X of Denmark

Boles, Ben Blue, Lena Horne, Marsha Hunt, Marilyn Maxwell, Donna Reed, Frances Rafferty, Margaret O'Brien, June Allyson, Gloria DeHaven and more. *Thousands Cheer* was directed by George Sidney and produced by Joe Pasternak. It is during the second half of the film, during a major musical revue, that the patriotic film comes to life.

Though lacking a substantive plot, as a WWII morale booster, *Thousands Cheer* hit the mark quite well. At that time M-G-M was the richest, biggest and most powerful studio, and it pulled out all the stops by parading out every one of its glamorous stars in a self-aggrandizing display of its support of the war effort. To see all that beauty and talent in one film alone was worth the price of admission—that, and the temporary cheer it brought to a nation at war. For these reasons, moviegoers were willing to overlook a lean script and simply sit back and enjoy some good fun and fabulous acts in a film called "a veritable grab-bag of delights" by the *New York Times*.

Thousands Cheer also was criticized for an absence of any memorable music, especially since it was called a musical. This was somewhat surprising in light of the fact that the music was contributed by such greats as Irving Berlin, George and Ira Gershwin, Lorenz Hart, Jerome Kern, Nacio Herb Brown and Max Steiner, with outstanding musical performances by Kay Kyser and his Orchestra, Bob Crosby and his Bobcats, Benny Carter and his Band and conductor José Iturbi. Overall, the score was popular, however, and Herbert Stothart, the foremost M-G-M film composer who worked on *Thousands Cheer*, received an Academy Award nomination for Best Music—Scoring of a Musical Picture. Additionally, it was technically spectacular both in front of and behind the camera, and the top-notch M-G-M production team was recognized for their work with Academy Award nominations for Best Art Direction—Interior Decoration—Color and Best Cinematography—Color.

Gene Kelly received high marks for his acting and typically vigorous, masculine dancing, albeit only in one number. It is in the first half of this two-part program that Kelly excels in his impromptu, mock romantic mop dance performance of "Let Me Call You Sweetheart"/"I Dug a Ditch." The story behind the now famous routine is a testament to Kelly and a mind that was as dextrous as his feet, capable of creating choreography in the least likely of places—combined with his joy of self-expression through dancing. As his character in *Anchors Aweigh* (1945) assures cartoon character Jerry Mouse: "Anybody can sing and dance. Well, anybody whose heart is big and warm and happy." As the mop dance story goes, Kelly spontaneously picked up a mop and thought up the dance—and ended up stealing the show.

As the USO show's emcee, Mickey Rooney introduces the acts and amuses with imitations of fellow Metro stars Lionel Barrymore and Clark Gable. A highlight of the film is Judy Garland's "The Joint Is Really Jumpin' in Carnegie Hall" and her boogie-woogie with film-debuting José Iturbi at the piano. Also

Dress and headpiece worn by Maxine for a dance routine in *Thousands Cheer*.

memorable was young Lucille Ball as one of the actresses examined by lecherous physician Frank Morgan of *Wizard of Oz* (1939) fame. Another highlight is watching M-G-M 1930s musicals queen of ratataps, Eleanor Powell, perform in her first color film, as adorable child-star Margaret O'Brien (the Shirley Temple of the 1940s) steps onto the set

Gene Kelly's onscreen paramour—costar Kathryn Grayson—was lauded by critics for her acting as well as her outstanding coloratura soprano voice in the first half of the film. After appearing in several supporting roles (as well as

Loper and Barrat pose for publicity photo for *Thousands Cheer.*

unfulfilled plans to appear in a film version of *Very Warm for May*), and once an aspiring opera singer, Kathryn Grayson landed her first lead role in *Thousands Cheer*. Maxine recalls:

> Kathryn Grayson was *wonderful*. She had the most beautiful figure and the most beautiful mouth—the way she would mouth her words. She was just lovely. A wonderful performer.

I was sad because he was such a nice person. In Hollywood you have to be very selective. A lot of those people get very carried away with themselves.

Maxine's considerate nature contrasted sharply with a lack of sensitivity exhibited by many Hollywood stars. Over the years she has witnessed a lot of poor behavior by some of the biggest names, including one display by Frank Sinatra:

We were on films in the same area of the studio. I was walking down the hall and there was this little guy cleaning the floor.

Frank Sinatra was right in front of me, walking down to his studio and I was walking with somebody. This guy, who was cleaning the floor, said: "Frank Sinatra! Oh, Mister Sinatra, I love your shows," and so on.

Frank said, "Get lost."

Those two words burned into me.

The poor little guy stood there absolutely shocked. I went over and put my arm around him, and said: "You know, he had a very bad day today. Don't be upset. He's just having some troubles."

He actually had tears in his eyes, he was so hurt. That was a terrible thing to do.

Aside from her close friendship with Ginger Rogers, one of Maxine's most enduring relationships in those years was with movie legend Clark Gable. By the time Maxine met "The King of Hollywood," Gable already had his most famous film, *Gone With the Wind*, as well as three Academy Awards behind him. In 1939, he would marry Hollywood's glamorous blonde beauty Carole Lombard, his leading lady from the one and only film they made together *No Man of Her Own* (1932), but she would perish in a plane crash only a few months after Maxine met Gable. His reputation as a lady's man was widespread—even after his marriage to Lombard, as Maxine attests.

Although he had all these affairs, Carole was very tolerant. She said, "Well, he'll come home." She had that attitude; she didn't mind it. Now that's very unusual for a woman. And he always did come home to her.

At the Copacabana in spring 1941, Maxine had met Ginger Rogers, who extended an offer to visit her in California. The first opportunity that Maxine and Don would have had to take Ginger up on her invitation would have been

Clark Gable and friend

between their Saratoga engagement and the Copacabana reopening in October. The circumstances were typically Hollywood:

> I met Clark and we started to go together. It was on and off in the beginning, then it got very nice.
>
> He was down-to-earth. Out there, you see a lot of temperament.
>
> I met him at a big party. He *hated* parties. I didn't like them very much either. Everyone is trying to be the biggest— and he hated all that. There was too much artificiality. People can't be themselves; even if you wanted to, you can't. It's a different world.
>
> I met him at this party and, of course, I was with Don. He didn't realize that I was with somebody and he asked me, "Shall we hit the road?"
>
> I said, "Oh, I can't. I'm with my partner."
>
> He said, "Oh, that's right. You're Maxine Barrat, aren't you?" He didn't even know who I was when he first talked to me. It was funny—a very funny situation.

Dancing with a Star

So I said, " I'm with Don, but I'm free for dinner."

He said okay; and that's how it started.

He did not like all the fanfare. It was so hard for him when there were certain appearances that studios required you to make. At that time the studio was the boss. Even though you were a big name, they were pretty tough on you and demanded appearances at certain places for publicity. It was to their advantage because it publicized the picture you were doing. Whenever he could get out of any, he would. Whenever we'd get a chance, we'd jump in his car and fly out into the country—way out somewhere where nobody even heard of Clark Gable. Out into the woods. Places he knew to get away because he couldn't take the pressure.

Of course you couldn't go out to a restaurant without everybody's "oohing and ahhing."

We even used to sleep in the car because he had this car where he had a bed set up that you could stay so we wouldn't have to put up with all the people in a hotel, which is hard. So he had this car all decked out very comfortably, I must say. It was this big car, specially designed for him.

Despite his fortune and fame as the biggest box-office star the screen had ever known or rumors and stories about his philandering, Maxine saw another side of Clark Gable's personality:

My dear, wonderful friend. He was so different from what people thought about him.

There is one story about Clark that gives an insight into his personality, feelings, and so forth. One night we were doing a scene for a film that he was doing the next day. He was so particular. He absolutely—unlike a lot of movie stars—knew his lines and everything he was going to do, say and feel. He worked through his script beautifully; that's why he was a good actor.

We're rehearsing this scene and then we stopped. We said, let's stop for a few minutes for a cup of coffee—take a break.

I said, "Clark, how does it feel to be king of this industry for another year?"

And he said, "Maxine, don't be silly. Next year someone better looking than I am and a better actor than I am will come along and that will be that."

Well, I guarantee you there aren't many people—and many men—in Hollywood who would have had that humble attitude. He was a very down-to-earth person and he really meant it.

News of Carole Lombard's ghastly and sudden tragic death on January 16, 1942 ticked out of teletypes and flashed over wires worldwide as Loper and Barrat were performing to packed houses three shows nightly at the Copacabana. "It hit him very hard," Maxine says. "He never realized how much he loved her until this happened."

Thirty-three-year-old Lombard was on her way back to California after selling defense bonds in her home state of Indiana when the plane in which she, her mother Elizabeth Peters, Otto Winkler (Clark Gable's publicist and close friend), 15 Army flyers and crew of three crashed into Table Rock Mountain near Las Vegas. Otto and her mother both had tried to persuade her to return by train, but Carole wanted to get home. There is speculation that she was worried about being away while her husband was filming *Somewhere I'll Find You* with sweater-girl Lana Turner. It was widely rumored that the film's co-stars were having an affair, which was fueled by a press that declared them "the team that makes steam." One day, Carole supposedly had walked on set while Clark and Lana Turner were doing a love scene. Flustered by Carole's stares, Clark's

Carole Lombard on a War Bond Drive

leading lady ran to her dressing room; when she came back on set Carole was gone. In Indianapolis Carole tossed a coin with Winkler and won; they would fly back. In the end, all aboard TWA Flight 3 were lost to the darkness of death.

Gable heard the news announcement of the crash over the public broadcast system as he pulled up to the curb of the Burbank airport terminal. Larry Barbiere, M-G-M's publicity man and Gable's friend, was waiting there and had already chartered a transport plane to take Gable, Mrs. Jilda Winkler and three other Metro men to the crash site. Gable's instantly aged, haggard

FIRST WITH THE NEWS
ESTABLISHED 1854   WATERLOO, IOWA, SUNDAY, JANUARY 18, 1942   THIRTY PAGES   PRICE SEVEN CENTS

CAROLE LOMBARD CRASH VICTIM

U. S. Sub Sinks 3 More Jap Ships

"Mr. and Mrs. G" in Wedding Picture

DIES WITH 21 OTHERS IN AIR PLANE FLAMES

NAVY ATTACKS ENEMY CRAFT IN TOKYO BAY

Report Japs Killed U. S. Missionaries

PAN-AM MEET PREPARED FOR BLOW AT AXIS

"Carole Died in Service of Her Country"

BRITISH BOMBS WREAK HAVOC ON JAP LINES

Tragedy Ends Idyllic Gable Marriage When Skyscraper Hits Mountain Top.

IS SOLDIERS, CREW OF 3 AND 4 PASSENGERS DEAD

---

face and sunken, unseeing eyes could only hint at the three-fold loss that he feared lie ahead: the woman who called him "Pappy," whom he adored above all others; a mother-in-law who had been the nearest to a mother that Gable, orphaned at 10 months, had ever known; and one of his and Carole's most trusted, dearest friends. All that remained were charred ruins—and the shattered lives of those left behind. Although Gable was able to carry out the instructions that his wife had requested for her funeral, he was broken by the loss, says Maxine:

He really loved her. This came as a terrible shock—and also, he felt guilty because he wasn't with her and she was flying home to him. That's why she took that crazy flight and ran into a storm. He went into a deep depression because he felt that her death was partially his fault.

There was talk about changing the ironic name of the movie Gable was working on at the time. *Somewhere I'll Find You* seemed like a cruel joke, but in the end the original title remained. A three-week trip to the Rogue River area of Oregon, where he had always found peace and tranquility, failed to console him. Consumed with grief and in seclusion at the desolate Encino ranch in the San Fernando Valley, where he had found so much happiness for a brief few years with his darling Carole. Gable began drinking heavily. A few of his closest friends tried to comfort him in his bereavement: Walter Lang and his wife; "Fieldsie," Carole's former secretary, confidante and closest friend; Lillian and Fred MacMurray; Liz and Norris "Tuffy" Goff; hunting pals Jack Conway and fellow Bakersfield Duck Club member Harry Fleischman and his wife Nan; Carole's immediate Peters family and Maxine. For Clark and Maxine, it was a love story about grief:

The Maxine Barrat Story 163

There were several people who tried to help him. One of his secretaries, a friend who was close to Carole—Fieldsie and Walter Lang were very good friends A couple of other people. Jack [Conway] and Harry [Fleischman]. Howard Strickley was the Metro publicity man; he wasn't exactly a great friend, but he was there from time to time.

So we had this group of people, mainly couples, who gave small parties, small gatherings. We could invite him to homes, nothing celebratory, but just to get him out of the house and away from his grief. All of us gathered around him to try to help him over it because we realized that he did need help.

After a while, he asked me, away from everybody else, if I would go to dinner with him that night. Somehow he picked me to go out separately because he didn't like a group as much as he liked being with me or one person. It was a very complicated situation.

I was at his ranch. I remember the veranda that went around *all* the rooms. We spent some time there; it was a good place to run away to—get away from things.

It was my job to help him get through his grief. In the meantime he was so tender and it was so wonderful with him. We had a beautiful relationship—a different kind of relationship. Our relationship was *so different*. It's even hard to explain.

He took comfort in me. I gave him something nobody else could give him. How can you explain that to anybody? It was love, but it was a hurting love. He was hurting so badly. He needed somebody and I filled the bill. That's why we became friends, even when I came back to New York—and we didn't see each other—he always called or sent flowers for my birthday or Christmas or something.

We had a very special kind of relationship. I helped to bring him out of his grief to the extent that he felt like living again. After I left, he started going out with other women again.

It was an experience in my life like I'd never had before or since. It was so unusual, but it was beautiful. So loving in many ways—and helping him get out of a loving situation in another way. I had a sensitivity for him that he needed; and for me, it was so natural. I knew exactly how to handle it; I knew just how to help him.

Within a week of losing his great love, Gable told friends: "There is nothing left for me in Hollywood now. I cannot stay there." For some time he had argued with Metro officials about enlisting, but they would not allow their biggest star to risk his life in military service. Now he looked for ways to get around his age and into active service, as had his beloved Carole, who was officially recognized as the first civilian to die while serving her country. On August 12, 1942, 41-year-old Clark Gable enlisted as a private in the U.S. Army Air Corps, Maxine remembers:

> Clark was impulsive. He joined the Army at that time. He just didn't care.
>
> He went into the service—and because I had suddenly become important to him, helping him get through Carole's death—I went through all of this with him personally.
>
> He went overseas. They had a special flight for him over to Europe. I saw him off when he left and I kept in contact with him while he was gone.

Meanwhile, Loper and Barrat had reached a crossroads. Don Loper wanted to pursue a career as a full-time haute couture designer; Maxine had her sights set on breaking into television. At the peak of their fame as a team, Maxine Barrat and Don Loper decided to go their separate ways:

> I thought when I was in movies at M-G-M that would be the ultimate. I would be thrilled to death and be so happy that I'd reached my goal. I reached it all right, but it was the emptiest

The Saturday Evening Post March 12, 1960

Photography by C. Robert Lee

Don Loper

Don Loper shows Judy Garland a piece of jewelry from his collection while her husband Vincente Minnelli looks on.

place in the whole wide world because where do you go from here?

I'd done it all. So now what?

As it turned out, Don and I decided we'd been together dancing long enough. You can't dance forever. So we decided we would split.

Don, of course, was a fabulous designer. He'd designed gorgeous clothes for me—and he went on to become a very famous designer to the stars. And I was lucky enough to have an offer to go back to New York and go into television.

Don Loper appears with Lucille Ball in *I Love Lucy*.

Don Loper had long nurtured a talent for fashion design, creating costumes for ballets, Broadway musicals and the Copacabana floor shows, as well as designing every garment worn by Maxine for their performances. While in Hollywood, he doubled in

STAR OF THE ICE... STAR OF THE DANCE... AND A WOMAN AGLOW WITH ROMANCE!

INTERNATIONAL PICTURES, INC.

presents

SONJA HENIE

in

"It's A Pleasure!"

in TECHNICOLOR

with

MICHAEL O'SHEA

MARIE McDONALD

BILL JOHNSON

GUS SCHILLING

Directed by

WM. A. SEITER

Produced by

DAVID LEWIS

SCREEN PLAY BY LYNN STARLING AND ELICK MOLL
An International Picture
Released through RKO RADIO PICTURES, Inc.

GOOD ENTERTAINMENT IS "INTERNATIONAL"

Don Loper was associate producer and choreographer for *It's a Pleasure*.

Ddancing and design, and he was an assistant to Arthur Freed, M-G-M musical director. Following *Thousands Cheer* (1943), he appeared in *Lady in the Dark* (1944), *Two Girls and a Sailor* (1944) and *It's a Pleasure* (1945). He designed costumes for movies and television, including gowns for Shirley Temple, Margaret Whiting and Patricia Morison, costumes for Joan Shawlee and wardrobes for Jean Wallace, Marlene Dietrich and Gracie Allen. Loper also was the costume designer for a number of episodes of the *Bat Masterson* TV series.

Loper's ability to combine his imagination with a knowledge of execution made him very versatile and he excelled in a variety of endeavors. He had a five-way contract with M-G-M: dance and film director, as well as costume, coiffure and set designer. His credits also include TV acting. He is probably best known to television audiences for his appearance (as himself) on the "The Fashion Show" episode (Season 4, Episode 19, aired on February 28, 1955) of *I Love Lucy*. Lucy wants to buy a Don Loper dress and he invites her to be a model at a charity fashion show, but the scratchy tweed suit that she is wearing irritates her sun-burned skin. Salesgirl Amzie (Amzie Strickland) brings out Don Loper originals worn by celebrity models Sheila MacRae (Mrs. Gordon MacRae), Brenda Marshall Holden (Mrs. William Holden), Jeanne Biegger Martin (Mrs. Dean Martin), Frances Neal Heflin (Mrs. Van Heflin), Marilyn Johnson Tucker (Mrs. Forrest Tucker), Sue Carol Ladd (Mrs. Alan Ladd) and Mona Carlson (Mrs. Richard Carlson) for approval by Ethel and Lucy. Lucy buys one of them—and sends her husband Ricky into a tizzy when he finds out how much she paid for it.

After Loper's M-G-M five-year contract expired, Loper decided to concentrate on fashion design. He and his partner Charles Northrup decided to open a chic boutique in Beverly Hills, which evolved over the years into a $25-million international fashion business. He opened his swank Rodeo Drive salon in 1946 and showed collections twice a year; soon thereafter he offered wholesale collections through department stores such as Lord & Taylor (New York), Neiman-Marcus (Dallas) and Carson Pirie Scott (Chicago). Today some of his clothing (bearing a "Don Loper of California,' "Don Loper Beverly Hills" or "Don Loper Originals" label), shoes and accessories, from handkerchiefs to toiletries, can be found in vintage dress shops and on the Web.

Loper's creations epitomized old-time Hollywood glamour, with prices that matched—as high as $25,000—and were worn by socialites and some of the biggest names in film: Ginger Rogers, Joan Crawford, Lana Turner and Claudette Colbert. While he mainly designed women's clothing, Loper also created men's attire and accessories. During a testimonial dinner for cancer-stricken Gary Cooper, Loper's well-known name was used in a quip by Milton Berle, "Sinatra would have been here, but he was trying on his new Don Loper wardrobe and the zipper got caught in the sequins." Today some of his iconic work from the 1960s is featured in the California African-American Museum, including a pink beaded stage gown with matching shoes and four other gowns designed for Ella Fitzgerald. The Fashion Institute of Design and Merchandising (FIDM) Museum, Los Angeles, has in its collection Loper pieces created in the

Connie Francis models a Don Loper creation.

late 1940s through 1957, including grey-and-black day suits, a green silk satin evening coat, a blue strapless ball gown with floral motif and a rose-pink evening ensemble of short coat and dress with floral motif. A woman's evening dress and coat, circa 1958, are in the collection of the Los Angeles Museum of Art.

Interior decorating was another of Loper's widely known talents. Among his inspirations was the green palm tree wallpaper at the Beverly Hills Hotel, as well as some special design touches found in the interiors of the Beverly Hilton in Los Angeles and the Roney Plaza in Miami Beach. All of his homes, from his early walk-up on Lexington Avenue in New York, where he lived when he and Maxine formed their partnership, to his grand home in Beverly Hills, which was adorned with Regency pieces and antique silver, reflected his artistry.

An underlying problem in Loper's personal life became apparent when he was arrested on suspicion of felony hit-and-run driving. A March 12, 1962 newspaper headline read, "Jerry Lewis joins chase for Loper." A three-mile chase by comedian Jerry Lewis and others ended with Loper crossing a double yellow center line and hitting another vehicle before angling across oncoming traffic, sideswiping three parked vehicles, jumping a curb and striking a bush. Although Lewis knew Loper, he was unaware of the identity of the driver of the car he was chasing. Lewis called police on his personal car telephone:

> I kept police posted on our position. I forced him to the side
> of the road and he stopped. I took the keys out of the car. I
> opened one door and a marine opened another. There were
> about four cars following.

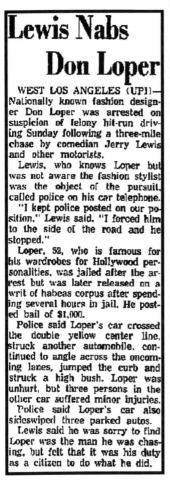

Lewis Nabs Don Loper

WEST LOS ANGELES (UPI)—Nationally known fashion designer Don Loper was arrested on suspicion of felony hit-run driving Sunday following a three-mile chase by comedian Jerry Lewis and other motorists.

Lewis, who knows Loper but was not aware the fashion stylist was the object of the pursuit, called police on his car telephone.

"I kept police posted on our position," Lewis said. "I forced him to the side of the road and he stopped."

Loper, 52, who is famous for his wardrobes for Hollywood personalities, was jailed after the arrest but was later released on a writ of habeas corpus after spending several hours in jail. He posted bail of $1,000.

Police said Loper's car crossed the double yellow center line, struck another automobile, continued to angle across the oncoming lanes, jumped the curb and struck a high bush. Loper was unhurt, but three persons in the other car suffered minor injuries.

Police said Loper's car also sideswiped three parked autos.

Lewis said he was sorry to find Loper was the man he was chasing, but felt that it was his duty as a citizen to do what he did.

Jerry Lewis was sorry to discover that the driver of the automobile he had chased was Don Loper but said later that he had felt it was his civic duty to pursue the erratically-driven vehicle. Loper was unhurt, but occupants of the car he struck suffered minor injuries. When questioned by an investigating officer, Loper explained that he had taken sleeping pills but unable to sleep, he decided to go for a drive. He refused to take a sobriety test. Loper spent a few hours in jail and was released on a writ of habeas corpus after posting bail of $1,000.

Stories about Loper's drinking had been circulating long before he became famous as a Hollywood-style impresario of fashion. He had started drinking as a teenager but was able to consume considerable amounts of alcohol without seeming impaired; however it became increasingly problematic as the years passed.

Don Loper died 10 years later on November 22, 1972 from complications following a lung puncture. He had fallen from a ladder at his home. He was 65.

PART III

METAMORPHOSIS

Chapter Thirteen
Between the Big Screen and the Small Screen

On a return visit to the East Coast in October 1943 Maxine rode for two days on the same train as Frank Sinatra, bringing instant notoriety to her already established celebrity status. That same month Maxine was featured in an article about Hollywood pin-up girls in *North Africa Stars and Stripes*, which crowned her "The Girl Whose Hair We'd Like Most to Have in Our Bombsight," a compliment to Maxine's desirously long locks.

Maxine worked in earnest at her modeling career. Her luxuriant hair was the envy of other models and the object of many successful advertisements:

> I had ads with every hair color and style imaginable.
>
> My hair was down to my waist. The reason was—in those days—they had all these exotic hairdos. And they loved my hair. Thank the dear Lord; I had the most beautiful hair in the whole wide world. It had a soft natural wave. It was a great blessing to me. The hairdressers *loved* it. They could do *anything* with it—and they did. At one time, I had "wings," of all things! And stovepipes.
>
> I also had all sorts of crazy hairdos for big fashion shows.

With our country still in the throes of World War II, Maxine once again donated her time and talents to the war effort. At the "Tuesday Night Canteen for the Merchant Marine," a formal affair of dance and entertainment held by United Theatrical War Activities Committee at the Ritz Carlton on Saturday, January 4, 1944, Maxine performed before the mayor and approximately 1,500 leading Army and Navy officials in New York. She also made an appearance at the Stage Door Canteen, which was acknowledged in a letter from the American Theatre Wing War Service, dated January 28, 1944:

> Miss Maxine Barrett [sic]
> New York City
>
> Dear Miss Barrett [sic],
>
> We want you to know how deeply grateful we are for your generous cooperation in appearing at the Stage Door Canteen recently.
>
> As you most probably know, the Canteen becomes the home of thousands of soldiers, sailors and marines while on leave in New York, and it is only through such assistance as

Maxine with her long hair, poses with her sister (right) and mother (seated).

you have given that we are able to continue serving the boys and brightening their visits to the Canteen. On behalf of the American Theatre Wing Stage Door Canteen, I want to thank you most heartily for your willingness to cooperate. We shall hope for a return performance very soon.

Sincerely,
[signed] James E. Sauter,
Chairman, Entertainment Committee
American Theatre Wing

After the breakup of Loper and Barrat Maxine set to work reinventing herself and putting together a solo act that showcased her talent as a singer. In November 1943, she returned to the nightclub circuit and headlined a bill with two young male dancers. Following her January 1944 war-effort work in New York, she headed to Boston. In early February 1944, Maxine was the featured attraction at the prestigious Fox and Hounds supper club in Boston's Beacon Hill. *Boston Daily Record* columnist George W. Clarke heralded her return to the nightclub stage:

> IT'S A LITTLE CONFUSING, but certainly one of the most interesting if not one of the most important bookings of the season, the engagement of Maxine Barrat at the Fox and Hounds…and so you will remember her better, she was the feminine half of the quite famous team of Loper and Barrat which stayed for more than a year at the Copacabana in New York. Now Don Loper, her erstwhile partner, is a big-shot in Hollywood, assistant producer, or something, and she, apparently, is out on her own…Well, whatever may be the reason for the breakup—if there was one—you can take it from here she is one of the most beautiful of all blondes, but with the face of a doll, and it will be most interesting to find out what she is doing as a single…The team played here many years ago, at the Mayfair, but that was before fame came to them at the Copacabana.

Clarke also commented on Maxine's social life:

> That handsome officer with Maxine Barrat over the week-end was Capt. Jim Riordan of New York City, member there of one of the oldest and proudest families of the Al Smith hierarchy… and Maxine, who is breaking in a singing act at the Fox and Hounds, was so excited over the special showing of "Lady in the Dark" at the Esquire because her ex-dancing partner, Don Loper, did so many of the dances with Ginger Rogers.

In October 1944, Maxine performed to the accompaniment of Bill Thompson's Romantic Rhythms at the Salon Versailles supper club in the new Café Parisienne in Washington, D.C., where she was touted "as lovely to look at and as delightful to listen to as she was in the picture, 'As [sic] Thousands Cheer'."

By December, Maxine once again was aiding the war effort. She was among the entertainers lined up by the American Women's Hospital Reserve Corps (AWHRC) talent scout Sgt. Doris Archibold for a show at Army Hall, City College of New York; former mayor Jimmy Walker's scheduled participation in the show was canceled when war bond sales claimed priority. There she

Maxine Barrat did her share for the war effort.

The Maxine Barrat Story

performed before the mayor and approximately 1,500 Army and Navy officials in the New York area.

During the month of February 1945, Maxine was part of a USO-Camp Show called "Hi Fellers" company (Unit #7) touring military hospitals and service clubs in the South. In March, she headlined the show "Chicks and Chuckles" (Unit #247) on another victory circuit. Her picture accompanied an article in the *Field News*:

> "Chicks and Chuckles," latest USO-Camp Show, featuring a load of fun and laughter, hits Will Rogers Field for a one night stand Tuesday evening at 8:00 p.m. at the Service Club. The gals, bless 'em, add charm, talent, grace, humor and beauty to the clever acts on this smart bill and many new tricks and novelties numbers highlight the show with dramatic, exciting suspense.
>
> Headlining the "Chicks and Chuckles" cast will be pretty Maxine Barrat, stage and screen personality, who will MC the show in addition to singing and dancing in her own original style.

In July, she was recognized for her participation at the "Seventh War Loan Rally" in Westport. "Everyone there was thrilled with you," praised Stanley Joseloff, Director of Radio at the BIOW Company, an advertising firm, in his thank-you letter to Maxine. "I am enclosing a check from Leo Nevens, Chairman of the Westport Seventh War Loan Committee, in the amount of $5.00 [as reimbursement for train fare]. I know it's quite a shock for you receiving such a large sum at one time, but try not to let it affect your way of living too much."

Several years earlier Allen B. DuMont had been granted an experimental license by the FCC for a television channel in New York City. By 1946, he would have his first regularly scheduled program on WABD, and the DuMont Network was incorporated the following year. Maxine was poised at the forefront of this new and promising technology.

Chapter Fourteen
A Pioneer of Today's TV Talk-Show Culture

Early television was regarded with some skepticism, some speculating it might be nothing more than a fad. Others predicted that it was the future of home family entertainment, as radio had been for a previous generation. Although World War II interrupted the development of this promising new medium, production of TV sets resumed immediately following the war.

In 1946, there were approximately 18 television stations in the country with only 44,000 (0.1%) households owning a TV set; by 1949, there were about 76 stations and well over 2 million (9.1%) homes with television sets, mostly in the larger cities. Regularly scheduled TV programs were virtually nonexistent even in New York City—the cradle of the new television industry—until 1948, when the prime time schedules of DuMont, ABC, NBC and CBS began to take the shape they would have in the early 1950s.

The William Morris Agency, which represented Maxine Barrat, was one of early television's foremost proponents. Electrical engineer and inventor Allen B. DuMont (pronounced DOO-mont), founder and owner of DuMont Labs of Passaic, New Jersey, had developed the first all-electronic television receiver available to the public in the late 1930s. In 1944, DuMont obtained a license for a New York City commercial television station, WABD. In 1946, a second DuMont-owned television station had been licensed and began operating in Washington, D.C., and experiments were underway linking transmissions of the two stations via coaxial cable. Technically, this was the nation's first television network. Bill Morris, Jr. of the William Morris Agency brought together DuMont Labs and Paramount Pictures, which then provided financial backing for the official creation of the DuMont Television Network in 1947. The fledgling network was competitively positioned with respect to another newcomer to the field, the ABC Television Network, but it did not have the resources of the well-established NBC and CBS brands, also vying for a place in the market at the time. The William Morris powerhouse was eager to add more of its clients to those who already had

Even in 1949, televisions were popular Christmas gifts.

their own television shows, notably Ted Mack, host of DuMont's most popular weekly program, Sunday night's *Original Amateur Hour*.

Maxine was a natural to join the ranks of other Morris topliners, many of whom—Milton Berle, Burns and Allen, Eddie Cantor and George Jessel, among others—were migrating from radio and breaking into this exciting up-and-coming entertainment medium. Maxine had international star appeal and a reputation that was founded not only in the world of dance-entertainment but also in fashion modeling—both disciplines requiring visuals to put herself across—making television an optimal medium to showcase her talent. With her rich, multifaceted background, Maxine was ideally suited to bring to a television audience amusements more varied and intellectually stimulating than the vaudeville and animal acts then popular on variety shows such as Milton Berle's *Texaco Star Theater*, Ted Mack's *Original Amateur Hour* and Ed Sullivan's *Toast of the Town*. WABD—Channel 5, the flagship station of the DuMont Television (originally licensed to Allen B. DuMont, hence WABD) in New York, offered Maxine a contract to host her own show premiering in the fall of 1948: "Television was very new, of course, at that time. I was thrilled about the offer because it gave me my next stepping stone."

The man directly responsible for luring Maxine to WABD was Robert W. Loewi. In 1939, Bob Loewi quit the William Morris Agency to work for DuMont, where his father Mortimer was Allen B. DuMont's executive assistant and chief financial advisor. Loewi had a background in dance, and he ran the Arthur Murray School of Dance shortly after joining DuMont. Loewi undoubtedly knew Maxine through dance connections and felt that she would be perfect to host a program, which he would produce. Not surprisingly, featured guests on other Loewi-produced DuMont programs were dancers, including the renowned Ruth St. Denis, who also appeared on Maxine's show. It was Loewi who called Maxine in California and initiated a conversation that would culminate in a contract for her own television show.

When Maxine got to New York, she met James Caddigan, DuMont's Director of Programming. Jim Caddigan and Mortimer Loewi were responsible for initiating programming concepts and scheduling that would steer the direction of all network television programming in the years to come—from morning news and "C-W-T" (clock-weather-temperature) that ran at regular intervals beginning at seven o'clock, to interviewing people on the street and providing the audience a camera's eye view of Madison Avenue to show the weather, rather than just talk about it on set. Although lack of money would prevent DuMont from developing his ideas properly, Caddigan's concept of offering visually oriented programs (food preparation, fashion, interior design) primarily for women would be copied to this day with enormous success on other networks.

Maxine actually made

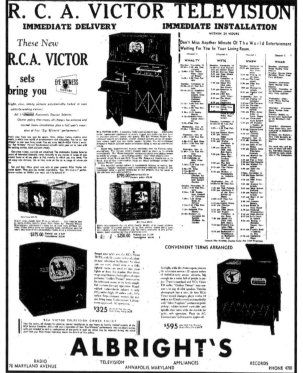

The television schedule for an evening in 1947, right beside the latest in TV technology—*Swing Into Sports* is listed in the second column.

her television debut a year prior, on December 22, 1947. She was a guest on DuMont's *Swing Into Sports,* one of the first regularly scheduled programs during television's formative years. *Swing Into Sports* was a low-budget live interview production that focused on home, style, sports and hobbies. Maxine and Latin and American dance proponent and studio owner Don Pallini were featured on a show that dealt with the dance. Her appearance on *Swing Into Sports* confirmed producer Bob Loewi's hunch that Maxine was as adept in front of a live TV audience as she was on a dance floor.

Maxine Barrat would become one of the very first female hosts of a network television show. It was a groundbreaking decision for DuMont—a milestone in Maxine's career—and a landmark in commercial television history. As host of DuMont's pioneering live TV talk-interview show *And Everything Nice*, Maxine would pave the way for the many women who would follow in her footsteps over the years—Barbara Walters, Oprah, Rosie O'Donnell, Ellen DeGeneres and so many others:

I had all the same things that they have now—absolutely.

I was probably one of the very first women to have a show like this—I was the only one that I can think of. They had comedy shows and other types of shows, but not necessarily a woman's show. It was groundbreaking. I guess I was a pioneer of sorts.

Television was just starting. DuMont was a very prominent network at that time, along with NBC.

The wonderful part for me was, I didn't know if I could do this after being a dancer—although I had done some comedy parts and I think that helped me to know that I had some ability, but it had never been tested.

Bob Loewi, the director, was the one who had the confidence in me that I could do it. So I asked him, "What am I going to talk about for 15 minutes?"

Also significant was the format of *And Everything Nice,* which allowed Maxine to ad lib. With its relaxed style and informal interviewing *And Everything Nice* set a precedent, becoming a forerunner of the celebrity talk show—one of the most popular and enduring genres in the annals of television:

Everything was live—even the commercials.

It was *all* ad lib. What I would do is make an outline, so that I would pick certain topics.

Dancing with a Star

Even the commercials were live in the early days of television—Maxine samples a Heineken on live TV.

I'd give an introduction: So-and-so was from [wherever], where they got their training and where they'd had some big shows. Whatever they told me that was of great interest, I'd put down—just a word or two, so that I would remember. I didn't write a whole sentence or anything—just a few words, so I'd remember what the subject was about. We didn't have teleprompters in those days.

I had three areas that I would touch on and the finale, showing the clothes.

So in a way I had notes that I could refer to, study the night before and get in my head. I'd be familiar with it all. When I got there the next day, I'd know about each person.

Keeping the right question coming, that's the trick—keeping it interesting.

And Everything Nice premiered on Monday, November 1, 1948. It was an important day in the New York City television market as it marked the debut of WABD's daytime programming. The *New York Times* announced: "*WABD Daytime Television—Now on DuMont's WABD Channel 5—New York's Window*

on the World—Open Day and Night." Officiated by Mayor William O'Dywer, the ceremony dedicating WABD's new all-day schedule was held at 3:30 p.m., followed at 4:00 by the premiere of *And Everything Nice*. Maxine Barrat was front and center on the horizon at the dawning of daytime television.

Producer-director-writer Bob Loewi conceived *And Everything Nice* as DuMont's answer to other TV fashion shows, such as NBC's *Paris Cavalcade of Fashions*, hosted by Faye Emerson and ABC's *Fashion Magic*, with host Marilyn Day. Initially *And Everything Nice* aired for 15 minutes during daytime hours. Maxine would chat with guests and present fashion and style trends for each new season from top New York and Paris designers. Maxine would break new

Maxine gives her audience tips on the latest fashions in hats.

ground in the ensuing months, enhancing the limited format of the competing fashion shows by including regular interviews of celebrities from the business, entertainment and political arenas on *And Everything Nice.*

Just as quickly as Maxine had accepted Bob Loewi's offer to host her own show on the DuMont Television Network, viewers responded in like fashion. Fan letters poured in from women expressing their enjoyment of Maxine's show, asking advice about various problems—how to add sparkle to a wardrobe, glamorize for a special evening with the latest Elizabeth Arden eye shadow, punch up a décor with color and so on:

> Guests like Dior, Elizabeth Arden or Caron always gave wonderful tips on fashion. It was always an interesting segment, because they would bring their models and we would see some of the clothes that would become the new styles.
>
> I had hairdressers—some of the top hairdressers that I had modeled for.
>
> Cosmetics. Elizabeth Arden—because I had modeled for her. The ideas she expressed on the show not only were glamorous but practical as well.
>
> It was all diversified. I would stick mostly to fashion, people from musical shows or opera, ballet, nightclubs—all

Maxine illustrates her motto, V for velocity!

these people whom I admired and had gotten to know quite well. We interspersed some politics, too. If there was a senator, for example, who was doing something special or coming into town, we'd have him on the show. We didn't limit it; we included anything that we thought would be of interest to our audience.

We played the field.

Each show began with a few pretty models frozen like mannequins in a simulated department store window setting, a gimmick devised by Maxine. As

Dancing with a Star

Maxine and models on the A.S. Beck stage

the orchestra struck up her theme song, Maxine would dance out and bring the mannequins to life by lightly tapping each one on the shoulder. A male voice narrated:

> To quote Maxine, what are little girls made of? Why, sugar and spice and everything nice. That's what little girls should be made of.
>
> Something nice each week on the Barrat models. We'll show you what the latest creations will look like at your favorite store. You'll meet Sugar, the best dressed mannequin in the fashion and entertainment world.

Aided by "Sugar" (Lee Klein), "awakened from her weeklong silence," Maxine would comment on the outfits of each posing, posturing model. While showing us "some things my gals are wearing," Maxine would describe in detail the beautiful shoes by A.S. Beck, one of the show's sponsors. She urged viewers "to be sure to ask your A. S. Beck salesman to see the shoes that were featured on the Maxine Barrat show:"

We had a *beautiful* studio—and wonderful people.

It looked like a Fifth Avenue department store window. Saks Fifth Avenue, for instance. I had five models. They were all standing posed, like mannequins, and I would set them in motion.

That was the opening of the show.

Then I would talk about the clothes they were wearing.

After the initial fashion commentary, Maxine would proceed to introduce and interview a celebrity who was visiting town. The format caught on—and Maxine found that she was a natural as a TV talk-show host:

For the first few months the show ran for 15 minutes, until I got used to handling it. Then I said to Bob Loewi, "Look. I need more time!"

So he said, "OK, what do you want?"

I said, "A half-hour show."

I found myself being able to talk to these people so easily. And we had all these *fascinating* people on with all different careers.

By March 1949 the show evolved into a prime time 30-minute series and the scope was broadened. Big-name celebrity guests were featured: bandleaders, chefs, opera and theater stars, politicians, newspaper critics and so on. One of her summer episodes featured a society fashion parade led by Lady Iris Mountbatten, glamorous cousin of the King of England, showing gowns of celebrated women of the 19th century. Maxine not only adapted to her role as a celebrity TV talk-show host, she excelled:

Later, when the show was expanded to an hour, there were 15-minute segments. Every 15 minutes I had somebody different on.

By this time I was swinging! I had six secretaries working for me at that point. When you get so much mail, you have to have people handle it for you. You also have to have people go out and make contacts for the people you want on your show. Somebody coming in from out of town, for instance—contacting them before they arrive, making arrangements before they come on the show.

I had all I could do to handle the show itself. To get it prepared, pick out the newest in color and design for the coming

country"), when he boasted that his Freeport, Long Island restaurant "served the best clams to be found anywhere." She jokingly begged to differ with the celebrated bandleader, known to millions by his radio, and later, television New Year's Eve broadcasts of his band and its theme song "Auld Lang Syne" played at the stroke of midnight.

Voice of Broadway

By DOROTHY KILGALLEN

The Broadway Grapevine

GLADYS GLAD, widow of Mark Hellinger, will invest some of her inheritance in New York real estate . . . Capt. Robert Glantz, one of the Army's bemedalled war heroes, and Betty Willis, a Sheraton Lounge peek-a-beauty, have been secretly married since April 11th . . . The movie companies are serious about their desire to produce a picture based on the life of Henry Ford . . . Maxine Barrat, who as part of the slick team of Loper & Barrat was one of the dancing darlings of the early forties, now in boniface of a cute spot in Mamaroneck called "The Westchester Clam Box" . . . A number of

The Clam Box

Maxine also plugged the Westchester Clam Box in an April 20, 1949 column, "Here's Looking at You!" that she wrote for a trade publication:

I saw you last Sunday, and you and you, in your gay Easter finery alongside of him in his new spring suit. How did your outfit look in the Easter Parade? Were you right in step with the fashion styles along Fifth Avenue?

You know, I saw a lot of polka dots, more polka dots and touches of bright yellow. These are definitely "musts" for spring. The newest shape this year is the slip dress. It has many virtues—it is inexpensive, easy to get in and out of, you can add your own short or long sleeve blouses (or sweaters) or if you prefer just add a short wool bolero—and don't forget scarves and scatter pins. One or a combination of these things can be added to your perfectly simple slip of a dress to give it great variety. An added feature and happy thought is the fact that it launders, packs and presses with a minimum of effort.

Another suggestion I heartily recommend is a coat-dress— it is the newest of new and a practical item as well. It can be worn two decided ways—one as a coat and again as a dress (be smart and buy one that buttons all the way down the front). I saw both of these styles at my restaurant, the Westchester Clam Box in Mamaroneck. Drop by some time.

But now it's time for the clothes. I mean—clothes—and before we close—I want to say one word of caution. Shop with an eye to the future. It is simple really, just keep away from fads and stick to classics, keep in mind the life you lead. Your good suit should be a healthy investment because if you buy it wisely it should serve many purposes (preferably a soft tailored suit that can be used as separates). If cleverly handled it can go with you any time of day or evening. Be sure to look in on the show next week for the latest in the lingerie spotlight. Until then, remember, here's looking at you....

Sadly, most kinescopes (professionally made movies taken of the image on a studio TV monitor, predating videotaping) of old DuMont shows were discarded. Only a single kinescope of *And Everything Nice* survives; the episode, which features avant-garde dance pioneer Ruth St. Denis, is archived and available to the public for viewing at the Paley Center for Media (formerly Museum of Television and Radio), New York City. It provides a good example of early television's experimentation, showcasing show host Maxine Barrat, one

of only a handful of women who worked in this male-dominated world.

Throughout this phase of her life, Maxine continued with her fashion career, modeling and hosting fashion shows at prominent hotels such as the Plaza and the Waldorf-Astoria, as well as at private clubs and residences: "I was always in such a whirlwind. At one point I had six secretaries just to keep things straight."

As star of her own television show, Maxine added cachet to any event; her participation was highly sought by sponsors and enthusiastically received by attendees. She also found time to travel, including stays in June 1950 at the Hotel de Crillon in Paris and London's Savoy Hotel, where she returned in December. She also made time for friends, including Clark Gable, who traveled to New York to see her:

> I went to California to see him, of course, but I also saw him in New York. He flew to New York to see me—I've forgotten now exactly why, but I remember he came. I was so surprised. I was in New York doing my television show—and he didn't even call me to say he was coming. He had a way of doing things like that—he all of a sudden popped up. Clark was like that.

Among Maxine's high-profile off-camera activities was serving as commentator for a fashion show benefit for the New Rochelle Hospital held at the Glen Island Casino on May 11, 1949. She also conducted a June 4th fashion show held in conjunction with a Nursing Care Foundation dinner dance and auction benefit at the Greenwich, Connecticut, Stonehedge estate of Mr. and Mrs. Sam Herman. On May 7, 1951, Maxine contributed her celebrity status as commentator for the Popular Price Shoe Fashion Show held at the Grand Ballroom of the Hotel New Yorker; Maxine lent a glamorous tone and tenor to the

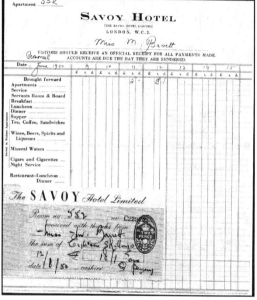

Maxine found time to travel to London—this hotel bill is a fond reminder of those trips.

90-minute show, which also covered fashions from both early fall and winter-into-holiday season. Maxine's ability to influence consumers was not lost on clothing manufacturers, who were truly appreciative of her participation in fashion shows. Jack Shor of Jordan Manufacturing Corporation wrote in a letter to her on October 3, 1952: "thanks and congratulations on a wonderful job at our Sea Nymph [swimsuits] and Givenchy show at the St. Regis, September 25th. Everyone thought you were swell."

Maxine also appeared on other television programs, including *Photographic Horizons*. Among the show's popular features was a succession of lovely models like Maxine, who posed before a variety of backgrounds. Home shutterbugs were invited to photograph them directly off their television screens. With

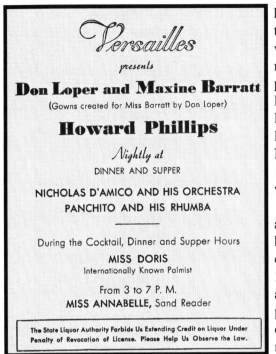

Maxine met her future husband Nick at the Versailles, where she and Don Loper had performed many times in the past.

her prominent reputation in the fashion industry, Maxine was highly sought as a guest model by host Joe Costa, president of the National Press Photographers Association. Maxine also was among host Harold Barry's guests on the November 11, 1949 episode of *Versatile Varieties*, a prime time variety revue set in a nightclub.

The same year that Maxine appeared on DuMont's one-hour TV original musical comedy series *Once Upon a Tune*, produced by Bob Loewi, another crossroad in her life presented itself. It was while dining at one of Manhattan's most elegant supper rooms one evening in 1951 that she first met charming and successful businessman Ralph B. ("Nick") Carter, Jr.:

It was one of the most important moments in my life.

We met at the Versailles. I was seated at a ringside table with a group of people for the opening night of a new show. Nick was with another group of people at a ringside table on the other side of the dance floor opposite us. He spotted me and remembered me because he apparently had seen me perform there; Don and I had danced at the Versailles.

Nick asked the maître d', "Who's that lady over there? I would like to meet her."

The maître d' came over to our table and told us. He knew me very well from my appearances there with Don. The maître d' said to me, "You know, Maxine, I would never do this unless I knew he was a very fine gentleman. He comes in here all the time." He wanted to reassure me that he wasn't introducing me to someone who wasn't known to him. Years later when Nick and I decided to get married, he sent us a telegram and signed it Cupid.

Nick and I didn't meet that night. When the maître d' told me that he wanted to meet me, I told him: "I'm going to be here for luncheon with some people on Saturday; maybe he would like to come by at that time." So Nick said he would be there and asked the maître d' to arrange for us to meet.

On that Saturday, I left my group and went over and met him. We made a date to have dinner together the next week. I think the first time we went out we might have gone to the Waldorf. From then, it took off. Not right away. It took time. We would go to dinner and the theater—he *loved* the theater, fortunately.

Nick Carter was smitten. Maxine had reservations. Although Nick hadn't lived with his first wife for some time, he was still married:

Dating a married man wasn't my cup of tea, but Nick was such fun.

I had just broken up with somebody—I had been engaged to someone else. I was ready for somebody new.

Nick ran the Ralph B. Carter Company, founded by his father, who had developed the Carter Pump in the 1930s to treat raw and activated sludge produced during water and wastewater treatment in industrial and municipal facilities. By the 1940s, the company had expanded its product line to include pneumatic ejectors and diaphragm pumps. Carter pumps were installed in thousands of industrial and municipal sludge and slurries applications. It was a very lucrative business. At the time that Nick met Maxine, he was commuting back and forth between his home in Miami and Hackensack, New Jersey, where the company was located. As their relationship grew, Nick tried to persuade Maxine to move to Miami in order to be together. As fate would have it, the television market was expanding; an opportunity arose:

New York was becoming such a rat race. And I'd worked so hard and so long that money really wasn't a problem anymore.

DuMont executives told me that another television station, affiliated with NBC, was going to open in Miami. So when I was asked if I wanted to go to Miami, I said: "Reporting for duty in Miami!" They couldn't believe that I actually wanted to go to Miami, but I was ready for a change.

WTVJ, a CBS affiliate operating on VHF Channel 4 since 1949, was the first TV station in Miami, the largest television market in the state. Once the

coaxial cable system brought live television to Miami, national network programs could originate. New UHF stations approved by the FCC sprang up all over the country after the freeze on television frequency allocations was lifted in 1952. WITV, Channel 17 (ABC/DuMont), became a UHF station licensed to Ft. Lauderdale just north of Miami and took to the air on December 1, 1953. Maxine was part of the nationwide television expansion when she became Florida's first TV weather girl on local WITV and subsequently on her own daily weather program, *Weatherwise - Maxine Barrat* on WGBS-TV, Channel 23 (NBC).

Carol Reed, who started at CBS in New York in 1952, is credited as the country's first female weather reporter, then called a weather girl. Carol Reed and others who followed were not professional meteorologists but came from various entertainment backgrounds. The weather girl was an early television

idea devised to imbue feminine allure to the dry subject of weather forecasting. Clad alluringly to spice up what many considered a rather dull topic, Maxine, for example, sometimes wore a bathing suit when she presented her weather forecasts.

Maxine was happy to put behind the hectic New York lifestyle and quickly settled into her role as Florida's first TV weather girl:

> I really didn't want to work very hard. The chaps at the weather bureau were all quite helpful. They spent hours telling me about fronts and barometric pressure and all that sort of thing.

Bill Byers, who got most of his material from newspapers and showed 16mm footage of local fires or car accidents, presented the news. Attractive model and weather girl Maxine might appear in a bathing suit, lovely necklace and heels and proceed to forecast the weather using a chalkboard for illustration—and she always signed off with a "V" as a salute.

People

Federico Pineiro, half of the Cuban comedy team of Garrido & Pineiro (known as "The Amos & Andy of Cuba") spotted at Don Julio's for dinner the other night . . . Paul Gray will be the clown on the Martha Raye show at the Beachcomber next week . . . June Garrett, the WMIE jazz disc jockey, is the new Miami correspondent for Downbeat . . . Maxine Barrat's back in town after filming a flock of commercials for television in Texas . . . Radio Winer's chef up at the Bonfire is now cooking up a new—to these taste

The American franchise of Heineken breweries sponsored the program. For the commercials a Dutch-costumed model would bring out a bottle of beer to give to Maxine. Maxine would pour the beer into a tall glass, smile into the camera and tell viewers how delicious it was. "But you weren't allowed to drink it on television," she noted.

After the show, Nick would pick her up.

The two UHF stations, WITV and WGBS, originally intended to serve the Miami area could not compete with the stronger, more far-reaching signals of new VHF stations that joined WTVJ during the mid-to-late 1950s. Most people could not receive UHF stations on their TV sets during the '50s, and both stations eventually failed. In 1956, the NBC affiliation went to Miami's new VHF station WCKT, Channel 7, which would remain the longtime NBC station in South Florida.

Maxine's *Weatherwise* program was well received by both viewers and sponsors, who recognized Maxine's star power and its influence on consumers. An example of sponsor gratitude was expressed in an October 4, 1954 letter:

Dear Miss Barratt [sic];

We have now been on WITV with your weather program each week since last May.

From the response which we have had from this weekly telecast, we feel that you deserve a word of commendation on the way you have handled this program for us.

It is usually not easy to determine results from any particular medium, but the offer of our Roman Meal booklets on your five minute telecast attests the fact that you have a large viewing audience. I do not know just how many requests we have had for these booklets, but I can say that we are well pleased with your part.

We hope to have you on this program for the present and foreseeable future, as we feel that we have spent our advertising dollar to a good advantage.

Cordially,
[signed]
Chas. M. Schwartz
Advertising Director
Fuchs Baking Co.

Some of Maxine's best friends were dummies!

By October 1955, Maxine was prepping a locally produced weekday morning movie-themed talk show to be aired by the soon-to-be NBC-affiliated WCKT. As a former Hollywood starlet, Maxine was considered ideal to host the program, *To See or Not To See*. Meanwhile, on Monday, February 13, 1956, she displayed her dancing talents on WITV's debuting *Mystery Disc Jockey*, originating from the Matador Room of the Seville Hotel; on February 23, she performed her interpretation of "Who's Got the Pain?" from *Damn*

Yankees. Another aspect of her television work that kept Maxine busy was making commercials. In July 1956, for example, she went to Texas to film a number of TV commercials.

While Maxine was in South Miami discussing the show with TV execs a week before *To See or Not To See* was scheduled to debut in March 1956, her North Miami Keystone Boulevard home was robbed. She had neglected to set her burglar alarm, and the error cost her the loss of $10,000 in furs and jewelry, including two diamond rings. The incident prompted her to adopt a new "bodyguard"—a wax figure named George whom she propped in the passenger seat of her car while traveling to and from work alone after dark. While she was still doing her late night weather show *Weatherwise,* she had several scares when driving to the Ft. Lauderdale studios of WGBS-TV. On one occasion she was flanked by two cars, forced off the road and approached by several men; fortunately they fled when she leaned incessantly on her car horn. She remembered how an *And Everything Nice* dummy named "Sugar" (off-stage voice of Lee Klein) had rescued her when she needed information about a gown on camera, and she decided to recruit another dummy to help her now—George, who "escorted" her every night with no further incident. He even gained celebrity status when Maxine brought him on to the set of *Weatherwise* every Tuesday night:

> I hoped that by having George in front of the TV camera with me, I could show other women who must work at night a solution to the problem that many of them have faced. A woman traveling alone is considered fair game by some unscrupulous people. As for myself, I solved the problem by this simple expedient. I let George do it.

Miami was a haven for celebrities. Both Arthur Godfrey and Jackie Gleason took their shows to Miami, so there was a pool of movie stars and other celebrities in the area for Maxine to draw upon. Beyond its being a favorite vacation destination for affluent New York society, politicians, entertainment stars and other celebrities, Miami hotels provided a steady influx of guests for her show:

> The big hotels there all had top entertainment at the time. They had the big stars—the biggest shows and the biggest names— and I had all of them! Whenever they came in to town—all the people who played in those various shows—they would invariably come and be on my one-hour show.

For *To See or Not To See*, Maxine moderated film and stage review panelists Meg Smith, Lillian Claughton, Art Green and Rear Admiral George McCabe;

Lucy, Maxine and Desi share some Hollywood memories.

also featured were celebrity guests. Maxine's subsequent *Miami Movietime* show also offered film entertainment along with sequences that included introducing upcoming Broadway shows, fashion and make-up tips for women and celebrity guests from all walks of life. Many of Maxine's guests were personal friends or acquaintances made during the course of her illustrious career. Walter Winchell in his syndicated column on November 7, 1956 wrote: "Maxine Barrat…is clicking on the Miami airwaves with her 'Miami Movietime,' a matineezy TV film feature." On the same day as Winchell's mention, Maxine hosted former *And Everything Nice* guests Lucille Ball and Desi Arnaz, along with *I Love Lucy* co-stars Vivian Vance and William Frawley:

> Lucy and Desi were *wonderful*. They were so easy to talk to because I knew them from Hollywood. Whenever they came into Miami, she told me she'd be very happy to be on the show. Lucy was so wonderful and a very good friend.

An interview that she considered one of the quirkiest was with the comedy team of Rowan and Martin. Straight man Dan Rowan and "dumb guy" Dick Martin had teamed up after the war and put together a comedy nightclub act, but it was not until the 1960s that they hit the big time with their highly popular NBC-TV comedy sketch program, *Rowan & Martin's Laugh In*:

Dancing with a Star

They were fun people. I didn't know too much about them. They came very late, and they didn't send me any information beforehand. So I said, "What am I going to ask you?" One of them answered, "We know what to talk about. We've been on enough interviews. Don't worry, Maxine, we'll make you look good!"

And they did! They fed me material that made it very easy for me to know *exactly* what they wanted me to ask them. They made it so easy for me.

It was great fun!

While hosting her WCKT program, Maxine continued to be active with fashion shows and fund-raising events. Saturday night and Sunday, January 18, 1958, assisted by Nancy Reed, Maxine acted as mistress of ceremonies with TV personality and game-show host Dennis James on the United Cerebral Palsy marathon, a 16-hour variety show at the Miami Beach Auditorium. Appearing on the Channel 7 televised telethon were just about everybody in show business who happened to be in Miami at the time, including Cab Calloway, Billy Eckstine, Buffalo Bob Smith and Clarabelle, the Ritz Brothers, Vic Damone, Phil Foster and Don Cornell. Shortly thereafter Maxine rendered her talents for "Les Artes et Couturier," held January 21-23, 1958, sponsored by the Miami Women's Chamber of Commerce. The event featured two major fashion shows were staged by renowned local couturier Claire Van Roy and directed by Maxine, who also supplied the commentary.

Maxine continued her own modeling career throughout this period, commuting frequently—often two trips in the same week—between her Keystone Point, Florida home and New York to produce and appear in television commercials. This demanding schedule prompted her to ask New York executives, "Why must I come up to you? Why can't you do this filming in Florida?" When she was told that this would not be possible due to the lack of modern equipment and qualified technicians in Florida, Maxine canvassed the area. She located all the services and facilities that would be needed—sound technicians, cinematographers,

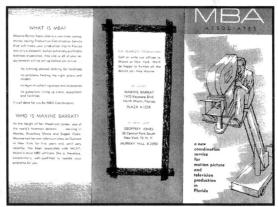

Maxine started a company, MBA, to provide coordination services for movie productions in Florida and also opened a New York office.

SINCAP PRODUCTIONS presents

FRANK **SINATRA** EDWARD G. **ROBINSON** ELEANOR **PARKER** CAROLYN **JONES** THELMA **RITTER** KEENAN **WYNN**

STEP UP AND MEET
SINATRA AS THE
BACHELOR OF THE
YEAR–ABOUT TO
LOSE HIS TITLE!

FRANK **CAPRA'S** "A HOLE IN THE HEAD"

IT'S A VERY FRESH,
VERY FUNNY,
VERY FRANK
CAPRA LOOK
AT LIFE!

COLOR by DeLuxe
CINEMASCOPE®

with JOI LANSING · CONNIE SAWYER · and introducing EDDIE HODGES (The Wonder Boy of "The Music Man") · screenplay by ARNOLD SCHULMAN · produced and directed by FRANK CAPRA · music by NELSON RIDDLE · released thru UNITED **UA** ARTISTS

make-up and coiffure artists, as well as dollies, sound equipment and soundstages. Maxine scouted for ready-made locations such as hotels, arenas, clubs and private homes—to make advance arrangements for out-of-town television and film productions. She formed "a coordination service for motion picture and television production in Florida" called Maxine Barrat Associates, with an office at the Coconut Grove Playhouse. There was also an office in New York run by MBA associate Geoffrey Jones. One of the first MBA jobs was the coordination of a fashion show sequence for Miami-filmed *A Hole in the Head*, starring Frank Sinatra.

Maxine also returned to the stage, not as a dancer but as the lead female role in legitimate theater, portraying artist Marion Froude in a production of S.N. Behrman's drawing-room comedy *Biography*. Although Maxine thoroughly enjoyed her television work, she missed performing for a live audience:

I went to Owen Phillips, Studio M's producer, and told him I was available for bit parts. He was casting for *Biography* and asked me to read a couple lines. I got real hammy; he slapped me down and when I had finished, Owen offered me the top role.

Biography opened a two-weekend run on Thursday, March 13, 1958 at Studio M Playhouse, Coral Gables, Florida. The entire action of the three-act play takes place in Marion Froude's New York City studio. The plot revolves around Marion's reaction to her lover's death by

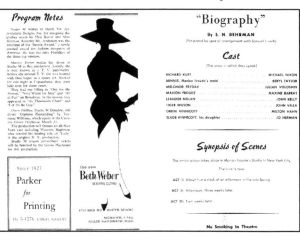

concealing her true emotions under a flirtatious demeanor; those around her in the play ridicule her, but Maxine's grasp of her part evokes pathos as she reveals her character's sincere nature. The *Miami Journal* praised:

> A new star is born!
>
> She's Maxine Barrat, local teevee personality…[i]n "Biography," now being shown at Studio M Playhouse, Miss Barrat vindicates Director Owen Phillips' instinctive evaluation of her potential as a legit artist. And this is her first stage play!
>
> In a many-faceted three-act comedy-drama by S.N. Behrman, Miss Barrat dominates the amusing play in the role of Marion Froude, artist and happy harlot with an enviable Bohemian outlook on life rich in tolerance that condones a casual concept that drives toward passionate promiscuousness.
>
> In the final analysis, the spirit of the play is captured by Miss Barrat's startling, sympathetic and magnificent interpretation.

At the request of Paul Hartman, who had known of Maxine's talents from her Loper and Barrat days, Maxine joined the cast of *Angel in the Wings*, which opened a two-week run at the Coconut Grove Playhouse, February 23, 1960. The delightful Broadway-style revue consisted of musical numbers, dances and humorous skits performed by Hartman, co-star Carol Bruce, Maxine and others. *Miami Herald*'s Ethel Tombrink praised: "Pleasant surprise, and we

Maxine and dancer-actor Paul Hartman on stage in Miami

hate to use the word surprise—it sounds like a left-handed compliment, was the fine performance of Miami's Maxine Barrat who's featured in several skits." Columnist Herb Kelly added: "Miamian Maxine Barrat, who used to be Don Loper's dancing partner, also makes with the comedy and joins with Hartman in a catch-as-catch-can ballroom bit. This is her finest local role so far." In April, *Angel in the Wings* opened at the Colonial Inn. In the cast was beautiful six-foot showgirl Mildred Hughes, who would be one of Maxine's dearest friends and traveling companion in the years to come.

Maxine's professional interests began to wane, however, as her relationship with Nick Carter became more serious. At this stage of her life she was ready to put aside her busy career and enjoy a more relaxed and normal lifestyle, entertain and travel with Nick. Finally she bade good-bye to her show on WCKT, modeling, acting and hosting fundraisers, and embarked on a journey as Mrs. Nick Carter.

Dancing with a Star

Chapter Fifteen
"Welcome to Heaven"

The fuselage of the prop plane glistened brilliantly in the intense tropical sun as it made its descent into the provincial airport on the island of St. Thomas. From the noisy, vibrating aircraft the newlyweds marveled as they would for years to come at the mystically lucid blue color of the Caribbean waters. Picturesque Charlotte Amalie harbor with its moored sailing vessels and boats bobbing idly came slowly into view. As the wheels of the plane touched down moments later, Nick turned lovingly to Maxine and said, "Welcome home, darling."

After a quiet wedding at Unity Church in Miami on December 2, 1960, Maxine Barrat and Ralph B. "Nick" Carter, Jr. had dashed off to New York for several weeks:

Maxine and Nick

> After the wedding, we took off for New York for our honeymoon. We went to dinner and the theater. We also had a lot of friends there who were giving parties for us.

As a wedding present, Nick had given Maxine a mountainside home atop Flag Hill overlooking the port of Charlotte Amalie, St. Thomas, U.S. Virgin Islands. Nick had owned the seven-acre property just south of Flag Hill's peak, at number 3E, before he had met Maxine. Now with Maxine in his life, he wanted to have a home built explicitly for her:

Nick had always wanted to have a home in the Virgin Islands. He had gotten a divorce from his wife.

He had bought the property sometime before. Then, when we had gotten together, he said the house was being built for me. I was in on the planning. He had started it and had some plans. Then he turned them over to me and said, "Would you like to change this, that or the other," which was very sweet.

Early in their marriage, Nick commuted between St. Thomas and New Jersey, as he still was actively engaged in his Hackensack business concern:

We had to fly from Miami into Puerto Rico. We stayed in Puerto Rico because we wanted to go to the gambling casino at night. We would stay overnight and the next morning we'd take what we called a "puddle jumper" into St. Thomas.

Before St. Thomas became popular, people would say, "You live on St. Thomas? Where's that?" It wasn't popular *at all*. Nobody even knew about St. Thomas. That was the time to be there. I was down there a couple of years ago and it was awful. We used to have a cruise ship come in maybe every two or three months. We'd go aboard, have a lovely dinner, dance to such lovely music and enjoy the ship. Today they don't allow you on the ship. All those cruise ships in on a tiny island. It's crazy. It's all blocked up—and the traffic! You can't make the streets wider. There's limited space. It is a God's blessing that I was there when I was. The place was *so* magnificent. We had all these beautiful shops with gorgeous china and silver and glassware—beautiful things from Europe. And there was no tax. We'd have these *huge* yachts come in just to go shopping—people would spend $100,000 in these different shops. It was a shopper's paradise.

At the time that the house was built, it was accessible only by cutting bush and riding donkeys. Its construction drew a great deal of attention—and the finished product equally as much. The Carters' St. Thomas house was open on three sides, allowing its

Maxine and Nick at a charity event in 1962

inhabitants to take full advantage of the breathtaking views. The plans included all the features that Maxine desired, including a spacious bedroom and master bathroom with a Jacuzzi and, as Maxine recalled: "The bath tub was turned into a waterfall." Years later the home was featured in a television documentary and offered viewers glimpses of all the interior amenities that Nick and Maxine lovingly had worked into the plans—along with its magnificent panoramic views:

> We had a *fabulous* view.
> You came into the foyer and a big living area. You could look right through the living area out into a beautiful garden. Beyond the garden was a teahouse, a gazebo, which was right on the edge of the mountain and looks out at the valley below.
> On the other side you could see where all the boats came around as they approached the harbor, coming in from the ocean and swinging around to the harbor. We had the whole view on top of the mountain.
> It was paradise.

Their design also incorporated provisions for part of the house to be converted into a theater. There were klieg lights, a multi-speaker sound system, a stage curtain and wardrobe changing spaces.   Nick was the resident sound and lighting technician. Maxine, of course, was the star:

> We had an idea for a theater. We turned a room into a theater. It was the kind of house that you could do that—it wasn't permanently set up as a theater. We turned the house into a regular dinner theater.
>
> We could clear out the main seating area and put up tables like you would have in a nightclub. We had an outside deck that overlooked the harbor, and we had a sunken bar; in the middle, between the main room and the bar area, which was huge and left plenty of room, we put on a show.
>
> We put up a sound system. Nick would say, "Everyone, take your drinks and please be seated. The show will start in 10 minutes." Nick had rewired the whole house so we had sound effects. We also had special lighting effects.
>
> We'd put on regular Broadway-style revues right there in our home. I had some friends, who lived there on the island, who were in the show. There was one girl who had a *beautiful* voice. She'd been a Broadway performer. She'd retired to St. Thomas, so she was in the show. She sang up a storm! There was another chap who had been a professional dancer. He and I became a dancing team. We did a number as a dance couple.
>
> Then I had my beautiful Millie [Hughes], who was a showgirl in theater. She did a wonderful number and sang a song. She had a huge string of pearls that started around her neck and she'd flip them and they'd go all the way down her body. It had a fabulous effect.
>
> We had a lot of good talent on the island, which is how we could put on an hour-and-a-half show. And the audience loved it. *Everybody* wanted to come to the show! We didn't put up any announcements because we wanted our friends there.
>
> Nick even had tickets printed up. You had to have your ticket! A boy collected them at the door. He stood at the top of the steps at the main entrance and collected the tickets as people came in.
>
> We did it very professionally. We did each show for three nights—and we had a full house every night!

Although their St. Thomas home had only one guest bedroom, they often invited a large number of guests, but that was never a hindrance or a problem. A 1972 production of *Follies* and *No, No, Nanette*, for example, involved accommodating

25 houseguests. Maxine had it all planned. As producer of her own TV shows and now those at Flag Hill, she was adept at problem solving. "We'll put them up at the Yacht Haven," Maxine told Nick.

Invitations went out to their widely scattered stateside friends, who would be responsible for arranging their own transportation to and from St. Thomas. The Carters would take care of the rest. Artsy informal follow-up bulletins providing flight schedules and encouraging casual attire were sent out after receipt of an affirmative RSVP. After being greeted at the airport with rum punches while their bags were collected courtesy of the Carters, guests checked in to the yacht club. After they were unpacked and settled into their new quarters, buses arrived to bring them for meet-and-greet cocktails with Maxine, Nick and some of their

In their house in St. Thomas, Maxine and Nick put on Broadway-style shows for their many friends.

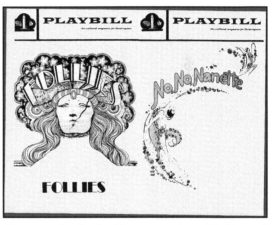

Program for the St. Thomas version of *Follies* and *No, No, Nanette* in 1972

island friends. For the duration of their stay, taxis or buses would be used to transport guests for island outings or to the Carter's home, where many of the evening activities took place

For many this would be the first time they would take in the breathtaking non-stop twilight views of Charlotte Amalie harbor from the home's huge open-air veranda high on Flag Hill. It was a diverse group of people, but all shared a sense of adventure and a friendship with their host and hostess. There was Maxine's dear friend, singer-dancer Millie Hughes, who later would go into the turban business and be one of Maxine's traveling companions. Jan Crockett—a former band singer and Miss Florida in the 1951 Miss America contest, who had appeared on *The Jackie Gleason Show* and *Jackie Gleason: American Scene Magazine* TV series—flew in from New York. Another member of the Jackie Gleason team there was set decorator-producer Phil Cusaco. Also present was

George Headley, head of Interama, and his wife, Olga, who entertained the group with her guitar virtuosity. Interama was a Miami-based international permanent exposition of the Americas—world's fair, trade fair and amusement park—that arose from the recognition of Miami as a growing commercial and cultural hemispheric hub, but it would never be fully developed.

Actress Peggy French, who succeeded Maggie Sullivan in the Broadway show *Voice of the Turtle*, was among the guests, as was her mother Virginia, widow of Ward French. French originated the concept of a permanent concert association on a non-profit membership basis—performers could rely on a network of municipalities with available funds to bankroll a season's concerts prior to signing a contract. He also founded Community Concerts, a provider of live classical concerts. Virginia and Peggy French were a hit when they arrived in Roaring '20s outfits for one of the festive gala evenings. Attorney Burton Keys, who attended with his wife Shirley, impressed guests with his vocal talent and made a commendable contribution to the evening's entertainment. Others on the star-studded guest list included: St. Thomas insurance magnate Ted Tunick; Olive Leeds, recent widow of "Billy" Leeds, heir to one of the country's fortunes through his father's late 19th-century tinplating process; big-game angler tournament record holder for a 845-pound blue marlin, Elliott Fishman; Ocean Reef Club (North Key Largo, Florida) sports fisherman Guy Brown and his wife Mary Maude; top model-friend from Maxine's modeling days in New York, Chrissy Roberts, who flew in from Baltimore; and Betty Sherwin, doyenne of Miami fashion and society-fashion director at Burdine's, a leading department store chain in the state of Florida and also a friend of Chrissy's.

Upon hearing that Nick had rewired the house to accommodate a special sound system for their shows, Betty declared: "Now it won't be so difficult for the next house party." Also attending: dermatologist Dr. Lou Skinner; Lady (Anna Lee) and Lord (Edward) Porter, college president and former consul general for Mexico; and Ralph Renick, a pioneer South Florida TV news journalist-anchor for Miami's WTVJ, channel 4.

With a spectacular view of St. Thomas in the background, Maxine puts her cast through their paces.

After dinner the *Follies* and *No, No, Nanette* cast of island performers took to the stage. Maxine and Nick had even had playbills printed up for the show, which listed the three selections to be performed from each play and the cast members. A highlight of the evening was an adagio dance performed by Maxine and local real estate agent Tom Moody, once a professional dancer. Their show-stopping personal expression of emotion and skill in lifting, balancing and moving received thunderous applause.

In the daytime, Maxine and Nick afforded their guests ample opportunity to take in the island's beauty and such activities as donkey rides and a stroll along the popular tourist destination of Magens Bay, with its protected three-quarter-mile white sand beach. Another treat was an all-day excursion aboard the Bomba Charger, a luxury charter boat that took guests to St. John's

Maxine waits for Santa Claus.

Caneel Bay and Virgin Gorda, the third largest of the British Virgin Islands. Included in the charter boat tour were stopovers for lunch, sightseeing, shopping and brief visits to the homes of some of Maxine and Nick's island friends, June and Al Brown, Judi and Arthur Witty and Louise and Elliott Fishman. It was a house party vacation that people talked about for many, many years, and by popular demand, the Carters would present other shows over the coming years, explains Maxine:

> *No, No, Nanette* was the first and biggest show; because it was so successful, we had other small shows like that, but those were for locals. *No, No, Nanette* was for bringing people from California, New York, Miami. The smaller ones afterward were for locals.
>
> We had all these people from all over and everybody had such a good time, we figured we'd keep the same pattern with the locals. Millie would come over to visit quite often anyway, but if she wasn't there, we just left out her part. We would call on our island friends who had been professionals, and they were happy to do it.

While Maxine would spend most of her married life with Nick in St. Thomas, the couple also passed many enjoyable days in Miami at their Cricket Club waterfront condominium:

Originally our home was in Keystone Point [North Miami]. Nick and two other men had taken this small airport and developed it. They decided to put in Venetian canals and beautiful homes.

We sold all the property at Keystone because we didn't want a big house anymore. At that point we moved into the Cricket Club.

They enjoyed a very active social life. When not entertaining at home, Maxine and Nick attended parties or theater, dined with friends or enjoyed time together or with friends on their private yacht: "Nick had yachts all his life. We had a beautiful yacht." Maxine enjoyed posing for pictures with their friends in the rear of their yacht or solo at the helm, smiling broadly while standing at the wheel. The Carters also passed many leisurely hours on their friends' boats:

Maxine and Nick spent many happy hours sailing on the *Who II*.

Our friend Marge and her husband had a big yacht at St. Thomas. They used to invite us out on it for yacht parties. We'd go down island and stay for a couple of days. Such fun.

Captioned pictures of them often appeared in local newspapers. When Nick surprised Maxine with a turquoise Lincoln Continental in fall 1961, the press was quick to report it. "The Lincoln was the first car he bought for me after we got married. That was a big thrill." They were often spotted in public, and newspapers offered occasional items about the comings and goings of the "handsome couple"—the pump king and his former TV hostess and dancer — who were regarded as one of the area's celebrity couples.

Maxine and Nick traveled extensively. On one of their many trips abroad Nick surprised his beloved wife with an unexpected gift:

We always traveled. We both loved to travel. We both loved the change, different scenery and different people. We traveled pretty much around the world. Cruises. We were always on the go someplace, adventuring.

This is a sweet story.

I had been talking about a Rolls Royce. I had seen one in Miami. One day I mentioned how much I loved that Rolls Royce. It was so beautiful.

So we get to London. I was upstairs in our room, and Nick called me from the lobby of the hotel. He said, "Please come down, I want you to see something. I see a very unusual Rolls Royce and it's parked right in front of the hotel. I just want you to see it because I know how much you like Rolls Royces." I came down and we went outside. I said, "Oh, that is gorgeous. I wonder what year it is," and I started asking all these questions. Then Nick pulled something out of his pocket, and said, " Here are the keys!" Nick had bought it for me! He had it shipped home. I was thrilled to death. What a surprise *that* was!

Overnight their tranquil lives were shattered. While sound asleep in their Miami home, burglars broke in and entered their bedroom. "I heard the door rattling," said Maxine. "The next thing I knew, they were in the room." Two men—one heavy-set and short, the other lean and tall—pounced on Nick and began to beat him viciously. Maxine could hear the loud blows to Nick's head, possibly with a handgun. A voice in her head screamed, "Get out—hide." She ran and hid in the garage. Assuming she had fled to a

Maxine poses with the Rolls Nick gave her.

neighbor's house to call police, the burglars abandoned their pursuit of her and fled the premises. Maxine rushed back to their bedroom and found Nick lying in a pool of blood: "They'd come very close to beating him to death."

Brain surgeries followed, but Nick was slow to recover:

He was beaten so badly.

He was very bad for a couple of years. He had ringing in his ears all the time. The pain would shoot up at any time. It was so bad that we'd have to cancel lunch or dinner or an engagement. He just couldn't handle it. After about two-and-a-half years, it finally subsided.

It was such a brutal thing to go through. It was so hard for him. He tried so hard not to show it, but I'd see him cringing. It was awful.

Maxine and Nick enjoyed yachting in Miami and St. Thomas.

The Carters were shaken further by a horrific act of murder that occurred in the idyllic U.S. Virgin Islands. On September 6, 1972, five Black Panther activists dressed in combat fatigues walked into the dining room of the Rockefeller-owned Fountain Valley Golf Club, St. Croix, cleaned out the cash registers and held up American tourist-club members and employees, demanding more money. When one of the hostages told them he had no money, he was gunned down; a shooting spree ensued, leaving eight slaughtered and three wounded. The F.B.I. and 300 U.S. Army troops were brought in to the islands to conduct a manhunt for the killers; house-to-house searches were conducted and virtual martial law was imposed. "The Fountain Valley Five" or "Virgin Island Five" as they came to be known, were apprehended, tortured to extract confessions and charged with the murders.

The sensational story created a media frenzy that was further exasperated when William Kuntsler, self-proclaimed "radical lawyer" and civil rights activist, came in to defend them. The five were found guilty and sentenced to eight consecutive life terms; the damage to Virgin Island tourism and real estate was devastating:

> When there was the tragedy in the Virgin Islands, the killings, we decided St. Thomas was going downhill. We wanted another place and decided to go to Costa Rica.
>
> We bought this darling little house. It was tiny but with a beautiful view on top of a mountain—35 acres. It was gorgeous with all the flowering trees—fruit trees with beautiful blossoms, then fruit.

August 9, 1979

Dearest Ginger:-

Thank You for Your note dated July 2nd. Due to our travels
it has just caught up with me.

I have written Al Lerner(as per the attached). I sure hope
that he can supply the answer.

We have had a rather hectic Summer-Particularly for Maxine
for I have had a balance problem(walk like I'd had a few
drinks to many)-We have been to every Specialist(and I have
had every test)to determine the cause. Net result=0.

Maxine has been really Terrific in carrying on my work as
well as the million other things She does. Ginger-I am a
very Lucky man to have found Maxine. Its now almost our 19th
Anniversary and she has made my life one of continuous Joy-
"Who could ask for anything more".
P.S.:I beleive she loves me too-as a matter of fact,I'm sure
of it-If She did'nt She would have'long since'kicked me out
along with my running series of problems.

We are now at our new Condo.in Miami. Maxine loves it here as
it takes a little of the load off.BUT-We both long to be back
at our Mt.Top St.Thomas Home(will be last part of September
and in New York 9/12 to 9/19th)

Hope our paths cross somewhere-soon again. We think(and talk)
often of You and Your Mother. Maxine never has forgotten the
great help You both were during Her'formative'years with Don
Loper.

If Maxine knew I was writing You She would join me in sending
our Love.

Stay Well and Happy!!

Nick

Even after all those years together, it looks as though Nick was still jealous of the lovely Maxine!

We held the Virgin Island property. You couldn't sell there after those shootings. The Virgin Islands were dead for about 10 years.

For a brief period of time, they were able to return to their idyllic lifestyle, but trouble was ahead for Nick. The problem began—as Maxine and Nick were approaching their 19th wedding anniversary—with small signs of loss of motor control, stumbling, coordination, perception, slurred speech. In an August 9, 1979 letter to Ginger Rogers Nick wrote: "We have had a rather hectic summer—particularly for Maxine for I have had a balance problem (walk like I'd had a few drinks too many). We have been to every specialist (and I have had every test) to determine the cause. Net result=0." Symptoms worsened. Eventually Nick was faced with a devastating diagnosis of a rare, debilitating spinal cord illness, which would ultimately claim his life:

We had a few good years before he started having trouble with his balance. A little stumbling, a slurring of words—then it got worse. When he got bad, we spent our time in St. Thomas, when he could go, then in Miami—back and forth. By this time, he was in a wheelchair.

We tried everything—surgery, acupuncture, chiropractic. We went to specialists all over the world. Nothing helped. He just grew weaker.

Nick Carter lived out his final days with his beloved Maxine at their peaceful St. Thomas mountain top retreat:

Dancing with a Star

I had taken him back to St. Thomas because we had help there. The doctors that we knew, who were our friends, were so wonderful. We had the best of care.

The house was so open. I could take him out in the garden. He loved it there. That's where he wanted to be.

When he died, I brought him back to the States. He was buried in a family plot in New Hampshire.

Ralph B. Carter, Jr. died on June 6, 1982; his daughter Patricia Carter Alders elaborates:

My father was buried in a small lakeside cemetery at Lake Warren that used to be called Warren Pond in East Alstead, New Hampshire. His memorial was held in Miami the year that he passed away with Ralph Renick giving the eulogy.

My grandparents bought the land in perpetuity. The Carter family had gone to Alstead in the summer for years. My grandparents owned two homes and a lot of land in the area.

George and Maxine in Bonita Springs

Maxine sought comfort in the St. Thomas environs that she had shared with Nick, grieving her deep loss. Unbeknownst to her, there was another island inhabitant, George Orenstein, who also was bereaving the loss of a loved one. Some mutual friends decided to have a dinner party so Maxine could meet the stocky, mustached South African ex-pat of German descent:

The island was so small at that time. We only had about 3,000 people on the island. It was tiny. You knew practically everybody on the island.

These friends of mine, who were also friends of his, decided we should get together. They had a special dinner party just for us so we could meet. They introduced me to him.

I had lost my darling Nick and he had lost his beautiful middle daughter. She got cancer of the bladder. She was there with him, visiting; she spent her last days on the island. It was so tragic. They did everything—they had her in every hospital, trying to save her. She was only 29.

At first Maxine and George found solace in each other's company; then they fell in love:

> We sort of held each other's hand. It was horrible, both of us having lost someone we loved so dearly.
>
> For about six months we just went around together. We went to parties, dinner—just helping each other through a tough time.
>
> About eight months later, we took a second look at each other and thought, *Hey, this isn't so bad!* That's when the romance began. George was quite a character. He had divorced his wife; they had lived in South Africa. He wanted to get as far away from her as he knew how. Somebody told him about St. Thomas. He came to visit the island, fell in love with it and moved to the island. Africa to St. Thomas—this is extreme! Everything he did was just that way. *Extreme.* He was the most fantastic character.
>
> He was one-hundred percent honest. If he told you something, you could bet your life on it. Even if it hurt you. If it were the truth, he'd say it. Brutally honest. That was George, and one of the wonderful things about him. He was so real. So down to earth.

A few months passed. Maxine didn't know whether or not she should keep the house and stay on St. Thomas. The home held so many memories of Nick:

> I didn't know what to do. It was in that first six-month period that I met George. I was there for several more years; then I sold St. Thomas. I moved permanently to Miami. That's where I was with George.

While Maxine and George were living on St. Thomas, they entertained at her Flag Hill home, where George cheerily greeted guests: "Welcome to heaven." Ginger Rogers came to visit, and she met George. "He and Ginger got along beautifully," says Maxine, "so that was fun."

Maxine and George had a wonderful relationship, but they remained an arm's length from marriage, literally:

I didn't marry George, but he asked me. He had a very bossy personality; he'd get bossy with me and I'd put up my right arm and stretch it out with my hand facing him, and say: *"Achtung!"* ["attention," in German] Of course that would break him up.

He had a very strong, domineering personality, so I thought, "I'm not going to put up with that." And I told him. I said, "George, you know you can't boss me about. I'll do anything to make things work fine, but you can't be bossy with me because I just won't put up with it." So I had it out with him from the very beginning of our relationship....

Ginger Rogers and George

I was afraid to get under that domineering personality. So I worked out a little deal with him so that when he started to get tough with me, I would do that with my hand up to his face, and I'd say, *"Achtung!"* He'd start to laugh and that would be the end of the argument. So that's how we worked it—and it worked beautifully.

I was so afraid to marry him. Any number of times I'd say, "You know I can't marry you." I knew it would save our relationship. I just knew it—and he knew it, too. He'd say, "Of course, you're right." If he put that ring on my finger and started to boss me around, our relationship would not last. I wouldn't put up with it. I could *not*. It's not my nature. I'm easy going and I'll do anything you want within reason. I'm flexible, *but I can't be bossed.* I have my limits.

I want to be married. I like that. I was brought up that way—to be married. But when you see that it isn't right, you have to lower the boom. It's not as important for me to be married. It's more important to save the relationship.

In fall 1983, they took their first trip to Europe. George had told Maxine about cellular revitalization therapy, which Maxine claims is the key to her vitality—and longevity. The CLP (Clinique La Prairie) extract treatment consists of injections of an extract from fetal sheep liver cells. The treatments are meant to slow and reverse aging as well as renew energy, eliminate fatigue, sharpen mental power and boost the immune system. The protocol requires a full examination (including skin and blood test to be certain that your body will not reject the extract) and administering of the extract on two consecutive days. Among the world elite who have sampled this rejuvenation serum are Winston Churchill, Margaret Thatcher, Charles de Gaulle, Pope Pius XII, Charlie Chaplin, Marlene Dietrich, Cher and others. Maxine attests to the effectiveness of the CLP treatments:

That is the secret to my longevity, absolutely. That—and my good health. When I see people in their late 60s, 70s, early 80s and how they are falling apart, I realize how much the treatments have done for me all these years.

George got me started on it. He was German; he knew all about it and he was doing it. He said, "You've got to start this, Maxine. This is one of the best things in the whole wide world. You won't have it over in America because doctors won't make enough money! But we all do it in Europe."

After I went with him the first time, we only went back once in five years. They don't tell you when to come back; they tell you: "You'll know when you need it. You'll lose energy and you're not up to where you want to be." So we didn't go for five years; then we went every three years.

Then I started to take Millie because she needed it so badly; we went every year. She went with me many times. When we'd get back, she'd call me every morning, and say: "I don't feel anything." *Every* morning she's calling me! I said, "Honey, you won't feel anything for two or three months."

She kept calling me anyway. "When does something happen? I don't feel *anything!*"

Almost into the third month, she called me one morning: "Maxine, I don't know what to do with myself. I have so much energy. I feel wonderful!"

That's exactly how it happened. And it's true. You don't feel anything right away. You're disappointed because you think you should feel *something*, but it doesn't work that way. When she called that day, I laughed so hard.

Back on the Scene: Maxine Carter, Epitome of Dynamic Youth

Maxine Carter, who epitomizes dynamic energy and youthfulness, and who, incidentally, throws the best houseparties in the U.S. of A., came over from Bonita Springs to visit with close comrades, **Millie Hughes, Lady Anna Lee Porter** and moi.

Long-time Miamians will recall that as **Maxine Barrett**, she was Channel 7's weather gal, who always signed off with a "V" as a salute. Before her TV career, Maxine starred in U.S. night clubs and in movies with her dance partner, **Don Loper**. She married **Nick Carter** and went to live in the Virgin Islands, where they led a glorious life until his demise. Many of us visited Nick and Maxine in St. Thomas. She and Millie, a showbiz whiz who is a statuesque monument to positive thinking, did the Europe scene this summer and a cruise as well. Millie now is in the turban business, which keeps her busy at her Boynton Beach residence. The laughter and reminiscences over luncheon at the Fontainebleau-Hilton were a gas.

Surf Clubbers have been riding the party waves ever since the formal opening when the dancefloor was crowded and the familiar faces as well as some of the new ones were "having a ball."

Missing and very much missed were **Lady Amy** and **Sir Arthur Gallow**, who, each year have entertained more than 100 guests at the annual event. Amy's fall last summer caused them to break the tradition.

Hosting several tables were **Illene** and **Dr. Marvin Isaacson**, who had just returned from a cruise on Celebrity Lines' newest ship, the *Mercury*. Illene was very chic and understated in black, accented with gold. Furs and jewels were everywhere. It was a chilly evening when furs warm the body and gems warm

the heart. **Ida Snow's** full length coat was spectacular.

Many dresses were in red, including **Dottie Meyers'** sparkly red. **C.J. Feimster** was smart in black. She was with fiance **David Rothrock**. Their wedding at the club is set for June. **Charlotte Jester** did a Victor-Victoria in a tuxedo. **Lorna Heisler** won "best dressed" honors in a pearl satin with satin roses nestled in the decolletage.

By Betty Sherwin

Lorna entertained at her apartment for **Marcelle** and **Jack Franks**, pals from London where she has a pied a terre. Following all this partying, this social dynamo took off for Canada to hit the ski slopes.

The sables, minks and chinchillas were also in evidence at **Michelle Headley's** holiday party but a cheery open fire kept the roses in the cheeks of the faint-hearted. Michelle looked stunning – as always – in a black sequin pant suit.

Every year, a feature of the Queen of Hearts Luncheon, is the clever program by **Bernice Melniker** but this year she outdid herself with "20th Century U.S.A." as a theme, artfully combining a diversity of acts including the fantastic Ziegfeld Follies "girls" who have a pact with Ponce de Leon. Community leader **Melvyne Sommers Zigman** was this year's well-deserved "Queen of Hearts."

Men's Opera Guild started the season with a cruise on the *Grandeur of the Seas* arranged by travel agent to the flitterati, **Earl Helfman**. The happy crew included **Ande Lippen, John Schmidt, Marie and Lewis Harms, Roz and Elmer Hurwitz, DeeDee** and

Bill George.

You may think you saw a lot of toys during the holidays but when it comes to toys, one must bow to **Larry Wilkinson**. At one time, he owned around 7000 of them, all collectors' items, and he runs a foundation dealing with antique playthings. Larry and **Suzanne** visited the White House with the Federal Arts and Embassies Program which puts arts including special toys in embassies all over the world.

Quote from the "Grosse Pointe News" (where the Wilkinsons have a home), "How does it feel to be a White House guest?" Answer: "Maybe a bit like a kid in a toy store."

And speaking of toys, etc. – the annual Bazaar and Dinner-Dance of the Animal Welfare Society's Women's Committee at the Surf Club was a winner. **Kay King** and **Barrie Sano-Mays** are experts at this annual event which requires hard work, much more than the usual charity party. The bazaar-cum-dinner dance is always a turn-on for the party animals who love animal pets.

Dancing with a Star

Even though there was significant fire and water damage, Maxine rebuilt her beautiful St. Thomas house.

> My stepdaughter and her husband went with me on the last
> trip that I took [2012].

When she returned to the United States, Maxine was met at Logan Airport by her stepdaughter Pat, who recalls:

> I met Maxine in Boston and drove her to New Hampshire
> in the fall of 1983. She was returning from Europe. This, I
> believe, was Maxine's first trip with George Orenstein and the
> start of their new life together. We placed my father's ashes in
> the little cemetery.

Maxine was in a new relationship and happy once again, but a distressing situation soon emerged. On Thursday, November 8, 1984, while Maxine and George were in California, a fire tore through her St. Thomas home, destroying about half of it. The blaze started after power had been restored following an outage of over 30 hours caused by high winds. When the power came back on, the home's burglar alarm sounded, alerting some of the help who lived on the property that the electricity had been restored. As the help rejoiced among themselves and started to return to their homes, someone saw smoke coming from Flag Hill 3E. They called the fire department immediately. Handyman Tony George attempted to douse the blaze with a fire extinguisher, but it was already out of control. The sounds of fire trucks could be heard from Charlotte Amalie far below, but the difficulty of maneuvering through the city's narrow

Firemen make sure flames are out in home after blaze on Flag Hill. No injuries were reported. The value of property damage has not been determined.

Daily News Photo - Terry Galvin

Flag Hill home burns when power is returned

By TERRY GALVIN
Daily News Staff

A home atop Flag Hill was hit by fire Thursday afternoon. The blaze that destroyed about half the home began as power was returned to it following more than 30 hours without electricity, witnesses said.

Fire Chief Carlton Dowe said Thursday afternoon no value of the damage or cause of the fire at Flag Hill No. 3E had been determined.

Despite a prompt response by two fire engines, a water truck and about 15 firefighters the house suffered heavy damage.

The first sign that electricity had been restored since high winds apparently caused a powerline problem at 1 a.m. Wednesday was the house's burglar alarm going off at about 1:20 p.m., said Mary Ohlsen, one of five people living

in three cottages on the property.

"We heard the alarm come on so loud that, if there was an explosion, we might not have heard it (the explosion)," Ohlsen said. "Just as we were rejoicing and going back to get our houses straight after being without power so long we saw the smoke."

Ohlsen said another woman living on the property, Marlene Nicholas, called the fire de-

See FIRE, page 12

Fire

Daily News, Friday, November 9, 1984

(Continued from page 3)
partment and a man who work on the property, Tony George tried unsuccessfully to stop the fire with an extinguisher

The women said they immediately heard the sirens of the fire trucks leaving Charlotte Amalie, far below, but that the trip through town and up Flag Hill delayed the firefighters' arrival.

The house on seven acres just south of Flag Hill's peak was

built by its owner, Maxine Carter, and her late husband 25 years ago, when riding donkeys and cutting bush was the only way to reach it, said property resident Ron Ohlsen.

Carter currently is I California, he said

The blaze occurred as the cottage residents were cleaning up after tropical storm Klaus, preparing for the planned arrival of guests of Carter's day.

Dancing with a Star

streets and up Flag Hill hampered their arrival. By the time the two fire engines and water truck made it to the scene to assist the dozen-plus firefighters in putting out the flames, considerable damage had occurred.

I was out in California with George visiting friends. They called us from the Virgin Islands and told us that the house was on fire. We stopped everything and flew back.

In the bedroom I had shirred curtains; somehow a fire ignited and the curtains went up in flames—and there went the house.

The help was there, but they were in their own cottages away from the main house. I guess they didn't see the fire until it was burning pretty badly. And, of course, being on top of that mountain, it was very hard for the fire engine to get up there.

We rebuilt.

Maxine was able to continue her globetrotting with George, visiting Southern Africa three times. Maxine adores animals and had many pets to keep her company, but in Africa she found a whole new group of animals to love. She has some vivid recollections of her first experience on the unknown and mysterious Dark Continent:

Maxine visits the local Humane Society.

We went to Africa together. Of course, he knew all the ins and outs. We traveled in a car, just George and me. We were driving, driving, driving. All of a sudden we were away from everything, all the homes, not a building in sight—in the middle of nowhere. Nothing. I said, "Do you know where you're going?" He got out of the car, put his finger in the air and said, "Oh, I guess we go that way." And he got back in the car. I was angry and I was laughing at the same time. Africa was so *huge* to me!

Halfway to where we were going, we came across some Masai [semi-nomadic people in Kenya and northern Tanzania]. These tall, tall people, with bodies about three inches wide—so skinny. We stopped to talk to one of them. George spoke three

Maxine expresses her innate affection for all animals at this local refuge in Africa.

Swahili dialects. George was in construction; he had built a huge building in Africa for the government to accommodate visiting dignitaries. That's when he learned to speak different Swahili dialects because of the help he had to construct the building. So this Masai native asked George for some directions. George said, "Honey, move your seat up and let him sit in the back." We drove him to wherever he wanted to go, but, of course, they don't bathe very often, so the odor wasn't exactly the most pleasant in a small car!

This was my first trip to Africa. It was *so* gorgeous. Once I got comfortable—knowing George knew where he was going since he'd been there so long. When you're with somebody the first time in a place like Africa, it's uncomfortable. I thought, "What if the car breaks down or runs out of gas?" It didn't bother him at all; he knew what he was doing.

In 1989, Pat Carter Alders and her husband Fritz accompanied Maxine and George on another trip to Africa:

Pat and her husband had never been to Africa. When she told me that, I said: "Would you like to go?"

Pat said, "Oh, I'd love to go!"

I talked to George, and said: "Well, we're going to Africa next month or whenever it was, why don't we invite them?"

So we invited Pat and her husband. We took a hot-air balloon ride and looked down on all the animals. We're looking down and the animals are looking up at us, like: *What is that thing?* It was so funny the way they looked at us with such quizzical expressions.

Nick's daughter Pat and her husband accompanied Maxine and George on a trip to Africa.

The balloon floated us over this beautiful scenery below. Then it came down in the middle of a field. There were animals all around us. They [the tour company] had guards on all four corners.

They set up a table and we had luncheon in the middle of this field with wild animals everywhere and guards all around. If any of the animals came too close, they would take care of it.

They had a big truck come out and pick us all up. When we finished breakfast, they put us in the truck and took us back.

When the trip was over, Pat said to me: "That was the best trip I've ever had in my whole life!" That's because it was so different. Everything we did was so completely different.

Breakfast on the plains of Africa reflected what Maxine meant by "everything we did was so completely different." On that morning, corks on bottles of chilled champagne were popped and long-stemmed glasses were filled—and refilled. Looking back, Maxine says: "That sounds like us! That wasn't unusual." When asked if that occasion pretty well sums up her life, she replied: "Yes. That's true." It also made a lasting impression on her stepdaughter Pat, who remembers:

> As I can recall, we got up very early—I think it has something to do with updrafts for the balloon, so early is better. It was my first trip on a balloon and I was a bit nervous. Maxine had ballooned before so she was quite excited to be going again. We skimmed the trees and followed herds of zebras, elephants and wildebeests. The African landscape is like no other. The pilot was fabulous. It was such a beautiful sight and very exciting.
>   Our landing was not a soft one. We had about seven people in our basket and for some reason we were a little off course. I remember landing on our backs and being dragged, bouncing all the way for some time. We then got out of the basket and walked to where the company had set up for a fabulous English breakfast and a glass or two of champagne.
>   At a museum for the poisonous snakes of Africa I learned that the mamba is the most poisonous snake in Africa and its habitat was right where we were walking. Needless to say I won't be ballooning there again.

An narrow-gauge locomotive built by Orenstein and Koppel in 1901 for the German Walluecke company.

On one of their European trips Maxine and George went to the region of Germany where George's family had their roots. The Orensteins had been part of a major mechanical-engineering firm, Orenstein & Koppel, abbreviated as O&K, which had been founded by Benno Orenstein and Arthur Koppel in Berlin in 1876. It specialized in railway cars, escalators and heavy equipment. With the rise of Hitler and imposition of Nazi programs, the Jewish Orenstein family forcibly had its shares in O&K sold in 1935. They fled the country:

> The Orensteins were engineers and builders. They did some wonderful things. They put in railroads, moving stairways—at the top you would see a big "O" and "K." The partner's name was Koppel.

Dancing with a Star

George and Maxine

The Orenstein family had had this beautiful castle just outside of Munich, where George had lived. I went to see it with him.

There was a huge, huge crystal chandelier. Underneath this beautiful chandelier were Coke machines!

When the war came, he and his family had to get out. He was so against Hitler. He had to take his family and run. They left for Africa. The Nazis turned the castle into a place for the soldiers to live.

Later it was turned into a youth hostel, and they put individual beds in the big ballroom. It was so crazy to see this gorgeous ballroom and the beautiful chandelier with the Coke machines underneath it.

Maxine reflects on her years with George:

He was a dynamite person. We had helped each other through that terrible time of mourning, never dreaming we'd fall in love. It lasted for 15 years until he passed on.

Afterword
"From Chocolate Bars to Caviar"

After George passed away, Maxine moved from Miami to Bonita Springs near Naples, Florida. She resumed modeling clothing and jewelry for both TV commercials and fashion shows, making hers the longest modeling career in fashion-modeling history. In returning to modeling, Maxine said: "I feel like I've come full circle." When she is not participating as a model, she is often emceeing a fashion show, as she brings a wealth of experience and cachet to events. She also appeared in a financial series on local television and radio, portraying the "dumb bunny" who makes bad investments.

Once defined by her friend Betty Sherwin as a woman "who epitomizes dynamic energy and youthfulness, and who, incidentally, throws the best houseparties [sic] in the U.S. of A," Maxine continued to maintain her active social life. She kept her strong ties with old friends, whether laughing and reminiscing over luncheon at the Fontainebleau Hilton Miami Beach with Millie Hughes, Betty Sherwin and Lady Anna Lee Porter or entertaining at her beautiful Bonita Springs home at 4324 Sanctuary Way. Maxine and Millie, described by Betty Sherwin as "a showbiz whiz who is a statuesque monument to positive thinking," often traveled together:

> Millie would travel with me lots of times to Europe, for example. I had so many friends over there. I'd make plans to visit and they'd say, "Oh, yes, bring Millie!" They loved having her. She had such a delicious sense of humor and she was full of fun. We had such good times together.

Aside from trips to Europe, Maxine still travels around the country visiting with relatives and friends:

> Every year I visit a darling friend of mine who has a beautiful farm in Ohio. It is gorgeous. There are horse trails through it. But I'm afraid to ride at this point. I don't want to get bumped off; I have to be careful. I used to ride bareback and just hold onto the mane. When I was a kid I used to love horses. I'd ride bareback and go over jumps—and fall off lots of times— because my legs were strong then.

Maxine is a true believer of good nutrition and exercise for maintaining a healthy and active lifestyle. She has taken classes in tai chi, Pilates and yoga. Her weekly regime includes regular exercise: "I still exercise a few times a week—that I wouldn't miss for anything." Maxine's spiritual life,

Maxine returned to modeling after George died.

opening her heart to God and remaining responsive to His divine presence, has played a significant role since she was a child. Her faith has been reinforced by occurrences that have been life saving. She still vividly recalls her first frightening encounter as a very young child, when she was submerged after the rowboat in which she was sitting overturned; Maxine heard a voice telling her, "Get on your hands and knees and crawl." She did, and it saved her life. One day while rushing to a modeling job in New York, she was about to walk out onto the street when suddenly she felt someone grab her arm. Out of nowhere a car came wildly around the corner. When she turned to thank the person who had prevented her from being struck, there was no one there. Returning home from a trip, she proceeded to the luggage area and then out to the curbside arrival area, but there was no one in sight:

> Out of nowhere a girl came along; she had no pocketbook, no luggage, nothing. She got a taxi, and I got in. When I looked back, she was gone. She had vanished.

This last trip that I took just recently to Europe, my stepdaughter and her husband went with me. This is interesting. I insisted that they go because both of them were having a lot of physical problems. I said, "You have many physical problems, so let's get rid of some." So I insisted that they go—and thank God I did. When we got over there—when they were giving him his examination before they give the treatments, they found out that if he hadn't been there, he would have been dead. That was a close call.

My intuition—I get these feelings and they're so *strong*. Every time I follow through on them, there's good reason. So spiritually—I've been led spiritually all my life.

On other occasions family and friends have made life-saving interventions, including an incident early in her career:

I lived in the Bronx and traveled to and from my New York rehearsals and shows by train, cab and foot. The trip was particularly exhausting, especially when the elements of rain and snow were added.

On one occasion, with plans to celebrate my mother's birthday the next day, I began my journey home after a full day and night of both rehearsing and performing. My house was situated on a high hill, a very difficult trek after a long schedule of work and a train-ride home.

This evening's journey was particularly exhausting because of the bad weather. The first lap in the ascent to my house was hazardous, with snowy slopes and icy patches. I slipped and slid with each forward step I tried to take. Though I tried to climb, leg fatigue and aching knees brought me down. I collapsed in the snow and fell asleep, chilled to the bone.

Looking back at what might have happened is frightening. Frostbite or pneumonia might have ended my career. But a neighbor, who had seen me coming home and laboring up the hill, saw me fall. He was at my side in minutes and carried me inside to warmth and safety.

My mother's birthday the next day was a great celebration.

Although raised Catholic, Maxine has found a new home at Unity of Bonita Springs church, which has played a big role in her life in recent years. As part

Even today Maxine keeps busy with modeling and her show "From Chocolate Bars to Caviar" based on her career.

of its regular Sunday morning worship service, Maxine presents an inspirational reading based on an original idea or reflections about an event that has occurred in the previous week.

With a vibrancy and beauty that transcends age, Maxine continued to remain active locally. When the Naples Players portrayed famous Hollywood film stars for a fashion showcase, Maxine was asked to be one of the participants. As she was looking through the racks of clothing, the color of one garment in particular stood out from all the rest. Instantly Maxine knew it was meant for her. It was a frilly turquoise gown that was reminiscent of the famous blue-feathered gown that Ginger Rogers wore for the "Star of Midnight" number in the Astaire-Rogers classic *Cheek to Cheek*. The audience was enchanted as Maxine moved throughout the room evoking the aura of her dear friend and mentor:

> They asked us to represent a movie star. There was a long rack,
> which was tightly packed. I saw a little turquoise sticking out,

so I thought, "I like turquoise; I'll see what it is." I pulled it out and it was a Ginger Rogers-type of gown. I thought, "Oh, yes—Ginger. I want to represent her."

I tried the dress on. It fit perfectly. I tried the shoes on. They fit perfectly.

They had the floor at the club cleared like a dance floor. So I danced out, and they had a professional dancer come out and twirl me around the floor. There were some steps on the side. I went up on the steps, and they stopped the music. The announcer said, "We understand that you knew Ginger in Hollywood for many, many years."

I said, "Yes, she was a very good friend of mine for over 50 years."

Then I looked up, and said, "Here's to you, Ginger, wherever you are." I blew her a kiss and danced off.

In early 2006, 93-year-old Maxine was invited to participate in the Whiteweld Foundation's "A Hot Winter Night" benefit in tribute to Ella Fitzgerald at Carnegie Hall in New York. Anticipating the trip back to the city where she had performed at such famous venues as the Plaza, the Waldorf Astoria, Radio City Music Hall and the Copacabana, Maxine said: "I've never appeared at Carnegie Hall. I'm thrilled to death. I think it's glorious."

Maxine and another Bonita Springs resident, Marilu Henderson, were among the 16 models from across the country who were part of the entertainment for the event's intermission show. Local director Joan Wood, who had done work for Carnegie Hall in the past, had brought the two models to the attention of event organizers. "We were both models and friends, and they needed people for the intermission," Henderson explained.

Patti Austin and the Count Basie Orchestra were among the featured performers for the Saturday, February 10, 2006 fundraiser. Maxine put her own spin on the intermission show:

We were doing modeling. But the one wonderful thing that I remember about it was how it turned out.

For some reason—and I'll never understand why—they wouldn't let us go on stage. They wanted us to go up and down the aisles—walk through the aisles—which was strange. We had these fabulous outfits on, but nobody could see us—only the people sitting on the aisle seats. So instead of modeling—the music was so good—I started to dance, and the whole audience started to applaud.

It didn't make any sense to me, so I figured to hell with this, I'm going to start dancing!

Patti Austin and the Count Basie Orchestra were the featured performers at a charity concert hosted by the Whiteweld Foundation. Maxine was part of the intermission show.

So I'm dancing up and down the aisle because everyone had modeled and no one could see them—it was a stupid thing to do. Why we couldn't go up on stage I don't know, but we couldn't. Modeling up the aisles? That's nuts!

So here I am dancing up a storm and the whole audience burst into applause. At least they could see *that*. It really was a funny situation.

A star-studded reception followed at Shelly's Restaurant, where such notables as Bette Midler joined them to support the cause:

The reception was fabulous, the food was fabulous—and everybody was in a good mood. Everybody was clowning around, having fun. Patti Austin, the Count Basie orchestra were there—that's why it was so much fun. It was party time—the show was over and you could have a drink. It was great.

For almost a decade, Maxine has been performing a one-woman show, "From Chocolate Bars to Caviar"—sharing her story from the poor and hungry days when Loper and Barrat struggled to find a job to their glory years. Offers to appear as the featured speaker for events have come in from various groups, organizations and clubs like the Naples Bath and Tennis Club (part of the Friends Lecture Series: *From History to Hollywood*, sponsored by the Friends of the Library of Collier County) that want her to entertain them with intimate stories about her illustrious career and the famous people she has met along the way—Lucille Ball and Desi Arnaz, Clark Gable, Ginger Rogers, Katharine Hepburn. No stranger to a microphone, Maxine keeps audiences spellbound with her fascinating story as images that correspond to her narration are projected on a screen. In recent years, however, a decline in opportunities to present her show reflects the nation's caution during times of slow economic growth. Organizations and businesses are reluctant to spend as freely as they once did:

Up until this past year, my Chocolate Bars shows have been sold out. Five hundred dollars is the asking price for a show but I will take less if it's a small church or group. I give the proceeds to charity—my church. I want to give something back.

Now groups are not doing anything. I've been having a hard time putting on any shows.

It's the same with the fashion shows. I did 12 fashion shows in 2011, but only two in 2012. I ask them, "What's happening?" They tell me, "People will come, but they won't buy, and we can't afford to put them on." People are hanging onto every penny.

In 2007, a Florida entrepreneur personally offered to fund a film of her life story, *The Maxine Barrat Story: From Chocolate Bars to Caviar*, which conveys the powerful dream, the grit and the thrill of success that collectively contributed to her inspirational career. Maxine was thrilled with the idea of having her career documented on film, but she was uncomfortable with the prospect of presenting her story in a monologue format. She decided to call upon Florence Henderson, a longtime friend, to assist her with the project:

I'd known Florence for many years. I knew her from New York. So I called her and said that I'd like someone to help me. I told her that I was going to do this documentary but I didn't want to be on camera alone. I need somebody to ask me the questions; it would be more interesting than if I just talk.

So she flew in to Florida from California. It was filmed at a hotel in Bonita Springs. We used the grounds of the hotel as a background because they were so beautiful.

Florence was a veteran in front of a camera—and the special bond between her and Maxine resulted in a dialogue rich in history, sincerity and warmth. Each was a prodigy with a master plan and an unshakeable drive to see her through the toughest of times. They also share an abiding sense of gratitude and a spirituality that has deepened over the years.

The youngest of 10 children growing up amid poverty in rural Indiana during the Great Depression, Florence's mother recognized early on her gift for singing. By age two, Florence had a repertoire of 50 songs, which her mother made her perform—and pass the hat—for folks at the local general store. When her mother left the family, teenaged Florence and her next oldest sister Babby were left living at home with their elderly, alcoholic, tenant-farmer father. With financial help from the parents of St. Frances School schoolmate Ruth Helen, Florence was able to fulfill her dream of auditioning for enrollment at New

Florence Henderson and Maxine Barrat working on the Maxine Barrat documentary.

York's American Academy of Dramatic Arts and subsequently attended on a singing scholarship.

Florence left school when she was offered her first job in the cast of *Wish You Were Here* (1952). Her vivacity and singing talent caught the attention of Rogers and Hammerstein, who immediately cast her in the last national tour of *Oklahoma!* Lead roles in other major stage productions followed. In 1970, she made her first feature film, *The Song of Norway*. Despite her many impressive acting credits, Florence Henderson is perhaps best known as matriarch Carol Brady in the long-running, smash ABC-TV sitcom, *The Brady Bunch* (1969-74). Florence went on to produce and host her own television show, *Country Kitchen,* and wrote her first book, *A Little Cooking, a Little Talking and a Whole Lot of Fun*; in more recent years, she has hosted *The Florence Henderson Show*, aired on the Retirement Living channel. In 1962, she became the first woman to guest host *The Tonight Show starring Johnny Carson* and has made numerous guest appearances on other TV shows over the years. Her quiet generosity and kindness is expressed through her promotional videos and contributions to the Sisters of St. Benedict (she was taught by a nun in school), her other humanitarian interests and her friendships; says Maxine:

> I called and told her about making the documentary. "I'd like somebody with me," I said. "Florence, would you be willing to do it? It could be a lot of fun."

She said, "Oh, sure. I'd love to."

She's such a pro; she's so good. It's so easy to work with Florence—like peaches 'n' cream. She remembered her lines perfectly. We had a vague script, but we sort of ad-libbed to some extent. As a matter of fact, she said: "I'm going to do some ad-libbing with you." I said, "That's fine with me."

We had a certain length of time and a certain pattern, whereby we were walking and talking in front of the camera. We started off sitting down and then we started to stroll. It was such a beautiful area, lovely trees, a waterway—all this around us. We purposely put it into that setting.

Florence made it easier for me because I didn't have to worry about her and what she was doing. I knew she would do what was necessary in her own fashion. I could be ready for whatever she was going to ask me.

She was here for several days. We were shooting for two days and she stayed over another couple of days. We went out on a little shopping spree—and had some fun.

Florence Henderson's genuineness shines through in her remarks about Maxine:

Just knowing you, I feel inspired. I think your life is an inspiration. I hope that *everyone* can get to know Maxine Barrat.

Florence Henderson and Corky Ballas on *Dancing with the Stars*

In 2010, Florence Henderson was approached by the producers of *Dancing With the Stars* to be among the celebrity contestants to appear in season six of the hit reality dance series. She accepted the offer and was paired with professional dancer Corky Ballas. Invoking the glamorous styles of Cyd Charisse and Audrey Hepburn, costumer Randall Christtensen created a sophisticated black ball gown with a sexily revealing side slit and dramatic red lining that was complemented in the lapels and cuffs of her dance partner's black tuxedo. Florence's facial loveliness was framed by the gown's crystal neckline, which gave the illusion of a stunning multi-strand necklace. Befitting her fame as Mrs. Brady, she and her partner performed a routine to *The Brady Bunch* theme song, receiving high marks for their efforts. In the same way that Maxine inspires people of all ages to stay active, then-76-year-old Florence hoped to send the same message; says Maxine:

> Good for Florence—she *would* do that! Give her any challenge and she will rise to the occasion. She's great.

Maxine enjoys watching dance reality shows, such as *DWTS* and *So You Think You Can Dance*.

> *Dancing With the Stars* and *So You Think You Can Dance* are wonderful in their own way. Some of those contestants are *amazing*. I applaud them for coming up with those routines in that short of a time.
>
> Don and I worked on our routines for two or three months before we perfected them in a way that we were happy with. I'm floored that they can do it—learn it that professionally—from week to week. More power to them, especially since one of the partners is not a professional dancer. That's amazing to me.

On October 27, 2007, Maxine joined former Copa Girls and stars in New York City for a Copacabana reunion held in conjunction with the publication of the book, *The Copacabana*. Flanked by the author, former Copa Girl Evelyn Peterson, production singer Terri Stevens, Copa Girl-production singer Julie Wilson, Copa Girl Susan Marie Seton and Copa Girl Joan Wynne, Maxine kicked up her heels in sync with them as photographers captured the moment on film.

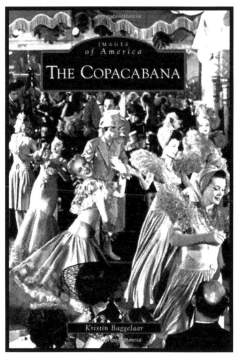

On Saturday, February 23, 2008 Maxine was the featured host of an Evening of Dance at the Center for the Arts, sponsored by the Art League of Bonita Springs of which she is a member. Its executive director, Susan

Bridges, enthusiastically welcomed an opportunity to deviate from a focus on painting and sculpture, and especially with the popularity and growth of its dance program—who better than to highlight it than a renowned professional dancer. Bridges said, "We have Maxine Carter right here in Bonita Springs." That evening, Maxine introduced various exhibitions by dancers from the local All American Dance Studios II. As part of the program Maxine discussed her long show business career, and the five-minute clip of Loper and Barrat's now famous "Tico Tico" dance sequence in *Thousands Cheer* was shown.

October 27, 2007 Copacabana reunion, from left to right, author Kris Baggelaar, Copa Girl Evelyn Peterson, Production Singer Terri Stevens, Copa Girl and Production Singer Julie Wilson, Copa Girl Susan Marie Seton, Maxine Barrat and Copa Girl Joan Wynne

Maxine continues to bring joy and inspiration to sell-out audiences with "From Chocolate Bars to Caviar," which generally includes a motivational message about the importance of an active lifestyle for all ages:

If you say you're through at 55, the body says, "Isn't that wonderful. I don't have to do anything anymore."

Say instead, "Look at all the wonderful things I've learned in the last 50 years; now, how can I apply all I've learned to the next 50 years?" It's true.

I would like to energize other people in their 70s and 80s. They get a mental block—they say, I'm 70—I'm over the hill. You have to make things happen. You can't sit in a chair and expect somebody to come by and pull you out of it.

I refuse to think about age. It's way out there somewhere.

It was once said of Maxine, "the light that radiates from her sincerity and warmth shines as brightly as the Florida sun." Perhaps the beautiful lyric from "All the Things You Are" by Oscar Hammerstein II—the song which provided the inspiration for the memorable Loper and Barrat performance at Radio City Music Hall over seven decades ago—best describes how she has touched so many, many lives: "You are the angel glow that lights a star."

Bibliography

Anderson, Jack, "About Television: No Hysteria Mars '58 Telethon," *Miami Herald*, January 22, 1958

Anderson, John, "'One for the Money,' New Revue Opens at Booth," *New York Journal-American*, February 06, 1939

Anderson, John, "Kern, Hammerstein Musical Sleek Amusement," *New York Journal-American*, November 18, 1939

Atkinson, Brooks, "The Play," *New York Times*, December 28, 1940, 16

Atkinson, Brooks, "Fable for our Times," *New York Times*, January 29, 1939, X1

Atkinson, Brooks, "The Play: 'One for the Money' an Intimate Revue With Sketches and Lyrics by Nancy Hamilton," *New York Times*, February 6, 1939, 14

Atkinson, Brooks, "The Play: 'Very Warm for May,' With Score by Jerome Kern and Book by Oscar Hammerstein II," *New York Times*, November 18, 1939, 23

Banfield, Stephen, *Jerome Kern* (New Haven, 2006)

Bell, Jack, "The Town Crier by Jack Bell," *Miami Herald*, December 26, 1960

Bourke, George, "Night Life," *Miami Herald*, October 6, 1955, 16-A

Bourke, George, "Nightlife with George Bourke," *Miami Herald*, February 18, 1960, 6-B

Butterfield, C.E., "Radio Shows Switching to Television; Some Dropping Radio Altogether," *Bee* [Danville, Virginia], October 3, 1949, 8

Candide, "Only Human by Candide," *New York Daily Mirror*, March 19, 1942, 22

Carruth, Gorton, *What Happened When* (New York, 1991)

Clarke, George W., "Man about Boston," *Boston Daily Record*, February 29, 1944, 16

Coleman, Robert, "Kern-Hammerstein Musical Tops in Tune; Story Lags," *New York Daily Mirror*, November 18, 1939

Crawford, Christina, *Mommie Dearest* (New York, 1978)

Daniel, Clifton (Editor-in-Chief), *Chronicle of the 20th Century* (New York, 1995)

Daniels, Robert L., "The Broadway Musicals of 1931," *Variety*, April 1, 2009

Dickstein, Morris, "Which artists will lift us?" *Newsday*, April 5, 2009, A41

Doane, Doris Chase, *Life's Astrological Assistance* (Arizona, 2003)

Farrell, Frank, *New York—Day by Day*, Scripps Howard and McNaught Syndicated, New York, New York, May 1, 1956

Fordin, Hugh, *Getting to Know Him: A Biography of Oscar Hammerstein II* (New York, 1977)

Freedland, Michael, *Jerome Kern* (London, 1985)

Galabinski, Andrea M., "Local model and actress journey to Carnegie Hall," *Banner*, February 11, 2006

Gody, Lou (Editor-in-Chief), *New York City Guide* (New York, 1939)

Gordon, Max, *Max Gordon Presents* (New York, 1963)

Green, Abel, "*Very Warm for May*" review, *Variety*, November 22, 1939

Green, Abel, "Night Club Reviews: Copacabana, N.Y.," *Variety*, December 10, 1941, 43

Green, Abel, "Night Club Reviews: Copacabana, N.Y.," *Variety*, February 11, 1942, 41

Griffin, Mark, *A Hundred or More Hidden Things: The Life and Films of Vincente Minnelli* (Cambridge, Massachusetts, 2010)

Hackett, Jane, *Ballerina: A Step-By-Step Guide to Ballet* (New York, 2007)

Harris, Warren G., *Lucy and Desi* (New York, 1991)

Henderson, Florence, *Life Is Not a Stage* (New York, 2011)

Holliday, Kate, "Loper Unites His Talents in One Career," *Ogden[Utah] Standard-Examiner*, May 9, 1943, 5

Johnson, Malcolm, "Café Life in New York," *New York Sun*, February 10, 1942

Kelly, Herb, "Maxine Barrat Has Butterflies," *Miami News*, March 5, 1958

Kelly, Herb, "'Angel in the Wings' Wacky and Slap Happy," *Miami News*, February 24, 1960

Kilgallen, Dorothy, "Broadway," *New York Journal-American*, November 25, 1941

Kilgallen, Dorothy, "Broadway," *Mansfield [Ohio]News-Journal*, February 25, 1942

Kilgallen, Dorothy, "Tales from Times Square," *Lowell Sun and Citizen-Leader*, March 17, 1942

Kilgallen, Dorothy, "Tales from Times Square," *Lowell Sun*, August 1, 1942

Kilgallen, Dorothy, "Broadway," *Mansfield News-Journal*, October 8, 1942

Kilgallen, Dorothy, "Dorothy Kilgallen," *Lowell Sun*, April 6, 1943

Kilgallen, Dorothy, "On Broadway," *Mansfield News-Journal*, September 16, 1943, 13

Kilgallen, Dorothy, "On Broadway," *Mansfield News-Journal*, September 24, 1943, 9

Kilgallen, Dorothy, "Dorothy Kilgallen," *Lowell Sun*, October 9, 1943

Kilgallen, Dorothy, "The Voice of Broadway…" *Oneonta Star*, July 15, 1948

Lockridge, Richard, "'Very Warm for May,' Jerome Kern Musical, Opens at the Alvin," *New York Sun*, November 18, 1939

McNeil, Alex, *Total Television* (New York, 1980)

Mantle, Burns, "Very Warm for May," *New York Daily News*, November 18, 1939

Martin, John, "The Dance: Art in the Cabarets," *New York Times*, December 24, 1933, X2

Martin, John, "The Dance: In the Theatres," *New York Times*, June 2, 1935, X6

Martin, John, "The Dance: Programs of the Week," *New York Times*, February 25, 1940, 114

McHale, Joan Nielsen, "Island Whoopee," *Palm Beach Life*, January 1972, 46-51

Meadow, Noel, "Argentina Explored," *American Dancer* magazine (New York City, March 1936)

Minnelli, Vincente, *I Remember It Well* (New York, 1974)

Musel, Bob, "From Window Dresser to Dancing Star," *Abilene Reporter-News*, February 2, 1942, 6 Neale, Wendy, *On Your Toes: Beginning Ballet: A Complete Guide to Proper Ballet Training for Pre-Kindergarten to Adult Beginners* (New York, 1980)

Peregrine, Anthony, "Deauville: a classy Channel resort," *Times* [London], February 17, 2008

Pollock, Arthur, "The Theater: 'One for the Money,' a Little Rightist Revue With Exquisite Settings and Swank Clothes Opens at the Booth Theater," *Brooklyn Daily Eagle*, February 06, 1939

Pollock, Arthur, "Very Warm for May," *Brooklyn Daily Eagle*, November 18, 1939

Pope, Virginia, "Scored for the Dance," *New York Times*, February 22, 1942

Pope, Virginia, "East, West Meet in Fashion Shows," *New York Times*, August 30, 1948, 20

Revell, Nellie, "New York Radio Parade," *Variety*, May 15, 1935, 43

Ritchie, Michael, *Please Stand By: A Prehistory of Television* (New York, 1994)

Riva, Maria, *Marlene Dietrich* (New York, 1993)

Roe, Dorothy, "Some H'wood Women Dress Pretty Badly," *New York Times*, January 22, 1954, 14

Rogers, Ginger, *Ginger: My Story* (New York, 1991)

Rose, Frank, *The Agency: William Morris and the Hidden History of Show Business* (New York, 1995)

Ross, "And Everything Nice," *Television World*, January 30, 1949, 6

Shaw, Arnold, *Sinatra, the Entertainer* (New York, 1982), 279

Smith, Meg, "'Let George Do It' And He Does," *Miami News*, c. March 1956

Schwarzer, Marjorie, "Bringing It to the People: Lessons from the First Great Depression," *Museum*, May-June 2009, 49-54

Sobol, Louis, "On the Manhattan Beat," *New York Journal-American*, December 21, 1960

Solloway, Lary, "Chatter: Miami Beach," *Variety*, February 8, 1956, 62

Straus, Rachel, "Russell Markert," *Dance Teacher* magazine (Mt. Morris, IL, 2007)

Strauss, Theodore, "Notes on Night Clubs," *New York Times*, December 04, 1938

Strauss, Theodore, "Notes on Night Clubs," *New York Times*, March 26, 1939, 134

Suskin, Steven, *Show Tunes* (New York, 2010)

Terry, Walter, *The Dance in America* (New York, 1956)

Tombrink, Ethel, "'Angel in the Wings' Packs Playhouse with Fun," *Miami Herald*, c. March 1960

Tucker, George, "In New York," *Frederick Post* (Maryland), February 6, 1942, 4

Twomey, Bill, *South Bronx* (New York, 2002)

Ultan, Lloyd, *The Beautiful Bronx (1920-1950)*, (New York, 1979)

Waldorf, Wilella, "Forecast and Postscripts: 'One for the Money' a New Revue at the Booth," *New York Post*, February 6, 1939

Waldorf, Wilella, "Forecasts and Postscripts: 'Very Warm for May' Arrives at the Alvin," *New York Post*, November 18, 1939

Watts Jr., Richard, "The Theaters: 'One for the Money,'" *New York Herald Tribune*, February 6, 1939

Watts Jr., Richard, "Very Warm for May," *New York Herald Tribune*, November 18, 1939

Weinstein, David, *The Forgotten Network* (Philadelphia, 2004)

Weiss, Pearl S., "Television Highlights," *Miami News*, 1956 (exact date unknown)

Weller, Sheila, *Dancing at Ciro's* (New York, 2003)

Whipple, Sidney B., "Very Warm for May" review, *New York World-Telegraph*, November 18, 1939

Winchell, Walter, *New York Daily Mirror* (syndicated column), May 20, 1941

Winchell, Walter, "The Man on Broadway," *Syracuse Herald Journal*, April 3, 1942

Winchell, Walter, *New York Daily Mirror* (syndicated column), November 7, 1956

Winchell, Walter, "Walter Winchell," *Port Arthur [Texas] News*, May 22, 1941, 4

Wozniak, Mary, "Dancer moves her feet," *News Press*, February 22, 2008, H.1

Yudkoff, Alvin, *Gene Kelly: A Life of Dance and Dreams* (New York, 1999)

Playbills and Articles with No Author Listed, in Chronological Order

—, "See the World's Most Gorgeous City, Rio de Janeiro," *Country Life*, January 1927, 15

—, "Rabbi to Bring Suit for Labrador Land," *New York Times*, March 13, 1927, E3

—, "Lincoln Loper Dies," *Variety*, January 12, 1932, 63

—, "Round the Square," *Variety*, January 19, 1932, 43

—, "The Patsy*" Playbill*, Jacob H. Schiff Center, Bronx, New York, May 1933

—,Obituary—Boura, Hypolyte Harry, *New York Times*, January 11, 1935

—, "Night Club Notes," *New York Times*, May 18, 1935, 20

—, "Music Notes," *Variety*, June 19, 1935, 66

—, "Music Notes," *Variety,* July 3, 1935, 40

—, "Night Club Notes," *New York Times*, October 19, 1935, 20

—, "15,000 in Times Sq. See Smoky Blaze," *New York Times*, April 1, 1936, 27

—, "Night Club Notes," *New York Times*, September 26, 1936, 11

—, "Night Club Notes," *New York Times*, October 10, 1936, 20

—, "Night Clubs," *New York Times*, October 24, 1936, 22

—, Display Ads, *American Dancer*, November 1936, 3-4

—, "Try A New Coiffure," *Sunday New York Daily News*, December 27, 1936

—, "Gaynor Premiere Adds Many Entries to Film Contest," *New York Evening Journal*, April 23, 1937, 22

—, Maxine Barratt [sic] photo/caption, *New York Evening Journal*, April 23, 1937, 22

—, "Chatter: London," *Variety*, October 6, 1937, 61

—, "To Rio and Return," *New York Times*, February 27, 1938, 78

—, "News of the Stage," *New York Times*, May 30, 1938, 8

—, "News of the Stage," *New York Times*, June 28, 1938, 23

—, "In the Summer Theatres," *New York Times*, September 9, 1938, 24

—, "Village Barn, N.Y.," *Variety*, November 30, 1938

—, "Plans for a New Revue," *New York Times*, December 12, 1938, 26

—, "Legitimates: Engagements," *Variety*, January 18, 1939, 52

—, "'One for the Money' Arrives Tonight," *New York Times*, February 4, 1939, 10

—, "One for the Money*" Playbill*, Booth Theatre, New York, 1939

—, "One for the Money," *Variety*, February 8, 1939

—, "Gossip of the Rialto," *New York Times*, April 2, 1939, 131

—, "News of the Stage," *New York Times*, October 6, 1939, 35

—, "Legit Openings: Very Warm For May," *Variety*, October 23, 1939

—, "'Warm for May,' 'Morning's at Seven,' 'The Hot Mikado,'" *Christian Science Monitor* [Boston], November 7, 1939

—, "Very Warm for May*" Playbill*, Alvin Theatre, New York

—, "Very Warm for May, *Daily Worker* [New York], November 18, 1939

—, "Plays on Broadway: Very Warm for May," *Variety*, November 22, 1939, 50

—, "Sobol Heads Loew's State Bill," *New York Times*, January 19, 1940, 22

—, "Picture Grosses: State," *Variety*, January 31, 1940, 9

—, "Radio City Music Hall," *Playbill*, Week Beginning Thursday, February 22, 1940

—, "Music Hall, N.Y.," *Variety*, February 28, 1940, 38

—, "Night Club Reviews: Hotel New Yorker, N.Y.," *Variety*, April 3, 1940, 42

—, "New Acts: Don Loper & Maxine Barrat," *Variety*, April 3, 1940, 47

—, "'All in Fun' Opens," *New York Times*, November 22, 1940, 29

—, "Doctoring 'Fun,'" *Variety*, November 27, 1940, 49

—, "Plays Out of Town: All in Fun," *Variety*, November 27, 1940, 50

—, "Murray Anderson Fixing 'Fun,' Baker Out," *Variety*, December 11, 1940, 49

—, "Shuberts Present New Show on Jan. 7," *New York Times*, December 24, 1940, 21

—, "'All in Fun' Set to Open Tonight," *New York Times*, December 27, 1940, 22

—, *"All in Fun" Playbill*, Majestic Theatre, New York, December 1940

—, "The Play: Bill Robinson Starring in Leonard Stillman's Musical Revue, 'All in Fun,' at the Majestic," *New York Times*, December 28, 1940, 16

—, "News of the Stage: 'All in Fun' Expires Abruptly," *New York Times*, December 31, 1940, 19

—, "Cabaret Bills: Copacabana," *Variety*, April 30, 1941, 64

—, "The Hotels and Night Clubs During May: Copacabana," *New York Times*, May 3, 1941, 21

—, "New Acts: Aurora," *Variety*, October 2, 1941

—, "Cabaret Bills: Copacabana," *Variety*, October 8, 1941, 48

—, "Night Club Reviews–Copacabana, N.Y.," *Variety*, October 8, 1941

—, "Cabaret Bills: Copacabana," *Variety*, October 22, 1941, 56

—, "News of the Stage: Other Items of Theatre," *New York Times*, October 27, 1941, 20

—, "Cabaret Bills: Copacabana," *Variety*, October 29, 1941, 48

—, "Cabaret Bills: Copacabana," *Variety*, November 5, 1941, 56

—, "Cabaret Bills: Copacabana," *Variety*, November 12, 1941, 54

—, "Cabaret Bills: Copacabana," *Variety*, November 19, 1941, 54

—, "Cabaret Bills: Copacabana," *Variety*, December 17, 1941, 48

—, "Cabaret Bills: Copacabana," *Variety*, December 24, 1941, 48

—, "Loper-Barrat Head Night Club Drive," *Variety*, January 7, 1942, 184

—, "Cabaret Bills: Copacabana," *Variety*, January 7, 1942, 186

—, "Cabaret Bills: Copacabana," *Variety*, January 14, 1942, 48

—, "Cabaret Bills: Copacabana," *Variety*, January 21, 1942, 48

—, "Night Club Reviews: Copacabana, N.Y.," *Variety*, January 28, 1942, 44

—, "Cabaret Bills: Copacabana," *Variety*, January 28, 1942, 48

—, "Cabaret Bills: Copacabana," *Variety*, February 4, 1942, 48

—, "Cabaret Bills: Copacabana," *Variety*, February 18, 1942, 42

—, "Cabaret Bills: Copacabana," *Variety*, March 4, 1942, 48

—, Display Ad—Gimbels: "Express Your Gratitude" Campaign," *New York Times*, March 22, 1942

—, "Treasurers Club Fete Sunday," *New York Times*, April 6, 1942, 18

—, "New York's Smoothest Dance Team," *Look*, June 2, 1942, 54-55

—, "N.Y. Copacabana Shut by Proser for Summer," *Variety*, June 3, 1942, 45

—, "Night Club Reviews: Blue Room, N.O. (Hotel Roosevelt)," *Variety*, June 10, 1942, 47

—, "Saratoga Sets Top Café Acts," *Variety*, August 12, 1942, 52

—, "Loper to Stage Copa But Won't Be in It," *Variety*, September 2, 1942, 49

—, "Joe E. Lewis at Loew's State," *New York Times*, October 2, 1942, 31

—, "House Reviews: State, N.Y.," *Variety*, October 7, 1942, 78

—, "Night Club Reviews: Blue Room, N.O. (Hotel Roosevelt)," *Variety*, October 28, 1942, 45

—, "Screen News Here and In Hollywood," *New York Times*, April 22, 1943, 31

—, "Chatter," *Variety*, April 23, 1943, 2

—, "82-Piece Ork Grinds On 'Rica Pulpa' Number," *Variety*, April 27, 1943, 8

—, Display Ad—*Thousands Cheer*, *New York Times*, September 5, 1943, X4

—, "The Screen: 'Thousands Cheer,' Lavish Metro Musical With an All-Star Cast, Makes Its Appearance at War Bond Rally at Astor," *New York Times*, September 14, 1943, 27

—, "Future of Pin-Up Girl Problem For After War," *North Africa Stars and Stripes*, October 30, 1943, 6

—, "Theatres: 'Thousands Cheer' Zippy and Colorful Musicfilm," *Evening Times* [Maryland], December 28, 1943, 11

—, "Midnight Party at Loew's State to Feature 'Thousands Cheer,'" *Syracuse Herald-Journal*, December 31, 1943, 13

—, "'Thousands Cheer' at a Camp Show," *Middlesboro, Kentucky, Daily News*, January 29, 1944, 4

—, "Sgt. Joan Roberts Heads 'Showtime,'" *Mail Pouch* (Vol. I, No. 9), December 1944, 1

—, "'Chicks and Chuckles' Sparkle With Fun and Entertainment," *Field News*, April 14, 1945, 4

—, Obituary—Loper, Miriam (mother of Don Loper), *New York Times*, September 15, 1947

—, "On the Radio Today: Television," *New York Times*, December 22, 1947, 42

—, Obituary—Boura, Monica (mother of Maxine Barrat), *New York Times*, March 24, 1948

—, "Programs on the Air: Television," *New York Times*, November 1, 1948, 46

—, "Programs on the Air," *New York Times*, November 5, 1948

—, "Programs on the Air," *New York Times*, November 18, 1948, 54

—, "Programs on the Air," *New York Times*, December 20, 1948

—, "Programs on the Air," *New York Times*, January 12, 1949

—, "Television Goes Daytime," *Radio & Television Best*, January 1949, 37

—, "Buttons and Bows," *Women's Wear Daily*, January 25, 1949, 8

—, "Programs on the Air," *New York Times*, March 2, 1949

—, "This Gay Group," *Daily Item*, June 6, 1949, 1

—, "Programs on the Air," *New York Times*, June 30, 1949

—, Display Ad—WABD Channel 5, "Maxine Barratt's [sic] Fashion show 'And Everything Nice' presents at 8:30 tonight the Society Fashion Parade led by Lady Iris Mountbatten," *New York Times*, July 18, 1949, 32

—, "Programs on the Air," *New York Times*, August 8, 1949

—, "Television tonight," *Bee*, October 3, 1949, 24

—, "Programs on the Air," *New York Times*, November 11, 1949, 48

—, "Programs on the Air," *New York Times*, December 25, 1949

—, "Programs on the Air," *New York Times*, January 1, 1950

—, "Programs on the Air," *New York Times*, January 8, 1950

—, "On Television," *New York Times*, January 15, 1950, X12

—, "On Television," *New York Times*, March 27, 1951, 41

—, "Fashion Markets Work With Volume Shoe Industry," *Boot and Shoe Recorder*, May 1951, 76

—, "Night Life," *Miami Herald*, October 6, 1955, 16-A

—, "For Week of February 12," *Miami Herald*, February 12, 1956

—, "For Week of February 12," *Miami Herald*, February 12, 1956

—, "Television Highlights for Greater Miami," *Miami Herald*, February 27, 1956

—, "Dialing Tips for The Best," *Miami Herald*, November 27, 1956

—, "Outdoor Art Exhibit Sponsored By Woman's Chamber Grows in Interest," *Miami Journal*, January 9, 1958, 8

—, Photo Caption: "Three to Get Ready," *Miami Herald*, January 19, 1958, 8-A

—, Display Ad—Channel 7 "Telethon for United Cerebral Palsy," *Miami Journal*, January 25, 1958

—, "Biography" *Playbill*, Studio M Playhouse, Coral Gables, Florida, March 1958

—, "Maxine Barrat, Personification of Perfection in 'Biography,'" *Miami Journal*, March 27, 1958

—, "Legitimate: Legit Bits," *Variety*, May 14, 1958, 60

—, "Angel in the Wings" *Playbill*, Coconut Grove Playhouse, Coconut Grove, Florida

—, "Angel in the Wings" *Playbill*, Colonial Inn, St. Petersburg, Florida, April 1960

—, "Jerry Lewis joins chase for Loper," *Bulletin*, March 12, 1962, 8

—, "Don Loper, Fashion Designer for Film Queens, Dead at 65," *Bridgeport* [Connecticut] *Post*, November 22, 1972

—, "Don Loper, Fashion Impresario To Hollywood Stars, Dies at 65," *New York Times*, November 23, 1972, 38

—, "Fashion Maker Don Loper Is Dead at 65," *Chicago Tribune*, November 23, 1972

—, "Nancy Hamilton Papers, 1962-1992: Biographical Note," Sophia Smith Collection, Smith College, 2005

—, "Cocktail Culture: The Glamorous Gold Coast Years from Prohibition to 1960," *Evergreen*, Planting Fields Foundation, Spring 2012 Newsletter, 3

—, Advertisement, "The Smart Glenview Women Series," *è Bella*, June 2008, Volume 1, Issue 6

Web site and Blog references

http://www.ancestry.com, re: U.S. Federal Census: 1920, 1930; New York Passenger Lists, 1820-1957

http://www.newspaperarchive.com

http://www.proquest.com (ProQuest Historical Newspapers: *The New York Times* 1851-2004)

http://www.ibdb.com

http://www.imdb.com

http://cinematreasures.org/theater/55/, re: RCMH

http://en.wikipedia.org/wiki/John_Robert_Powers

http://en.wikipedia.org/wiki/Ginger_Rogers

http://www.johnrobertpowers.net/newsviewer.asp?image=HowtoHavepg11.jpg

http://www.johnrobertpowers.net/newsviewer.asp?image=HowtoHavepg14.jpg

http://www.dance.lovetoknow.com/Ballet_Movements

http://www.astro.com/astro-databank/Loper,_Don, re: Don Loper

http://streetsofwashington.blogspot.com/2010/03/magnificent-raleigh-hotel.html, re: Raleigh Hotel, Washington, D.C.

http://www.oldandsold.com/articles06/new-york-city-77.shtml, re: Mary Anita Loos

http://www.hollywoodreporter.com/hr/content_display/features/people e3i9b4549028bac41bacd751f88057d92fd

http://www.youtube.com/watch?v=lFMmjKWQUqM (Ginger Rogers interview)

http://viviantalksgingerrogers.blogspot.com/

http://dearmrgable.com

http://www.murphsplace.com/lombard/end.html

http://www.jgdb.co, (Judy Garland Database), re: *Thousands Cheer* Program [1:37] "Tico Tico"

http://www.www.FIDMmuseum.org

http://www.nationalmuseum.af.mil

http://www.earlytelevision.org/us_tv_sets.html, re: Estimated U.S. TV Sets and Stations

http://www.rogersimmons.com, re: Florida TV History

http://hometown.aol.com, re: Women and Weather

http://articles.sun-sentinel.com/1986-11-23/features/8603120646_1_maxine-cruise-ships-george groups.yahoo.com/group/songbird/

http://www.carterpump.com/about_carter_pump.php

http://www.tehamaconcertseries.org/history

http://thinkexist.com/quotes/florence_henderson/2.html

Theater Credits

The Patsy (Jacob. H. Schiff Center, Bronx, May 20-21, 1933)
Cast (in order of appearance): Rose Trimmer (Mrs. Harrington), Gerald Meresco (Mr. Harrington), Ruth Weiss (Grace Harrington), **Maxine Boura** (Patricia Harrington), Buddy McCoy (Billy Caldwell), Howard Fensten (Tony Anderson), Sylvia London (Sadie Buchanan), Mario Sassone (Francis Patrick O'Flaherty), Mario Sassone ("Trip" Busty)
Credits: Staged by Gerald Meresco. Three acts.

One for the Money (Booth Theatre, February 4, 1939-May 27, 1939)
Opening Night Cast: William Archibald, **Maxine Barrat** (Client, Friend, Lucy Timpkin, Secretary, the Archduchess, Ensemble), Philip Bourneuf, Frances Comstock, Alfred Drake, Brenda Forbes, Nadine Gae, Nancy Hamilton, Ray Kavanaugh and his orchestra, Gene Kelly, George Lloyd, Don Loper, Ruth Matteson, Grace McDonald, Nell O'Day, Robert Smith, Keenan Wynn
Credits: Producers: Gertrude Macy and Stanley Gilkey by arrangement with Robert F. Cutler; Sketches and Lyrics: Nancy Hamilton; Music: Morgan Lewis; Musical Arranger: Hans Spialek; Vocal Arranger: Hugh Martin; Director/Lighting Designer: John Murray Anderson; Choreographer: Robert Alton; Sketches Staged by Edward Clarke Lilley; Scenic and Costume Designer: Raoul Pène Du Bois. Two acts; 21 scenes. Total performances: 132

Very Warm for May (Alvin Theatre, November 17, 1939-January 6, 1940)
Opening Night Cast: June Allyson, Dolores Anderson, Eve Arden, **Maxine Barrat** (Honey), Seldon Bennett, Beulah Blake, Helen Bliss, Donald Brian, Virginia Card, Peter Chambers, Andre Charise, William Collins, Sally Craven, Milton DeLugg, Helen Donovan, Eleanor Eberle, Frank Egan, Vera-Ellen, Bruce Evans, Marshal Fisher, Miriam Franklyn, Kate Friedlich, Ralph Hansell, Claire Harvey, Louis Hightower, Avon Long, Walter Long, Don Loper, Ethel Lynn, Matt Malneck, Charles Marlowe, Ray Mayer, Grace McDonald, Len Mence, Frances Mercer, Rudy Miller, Russ Morhoff, Kay Picture, Jean Plummer, Mary Louise Quevli, Richard Quine, Joseph Quintile, Pamela Randell, Jack Seymour, Robert Shackleton, Hollace Shaw, Hiram Sherman, Max Showalter, Ralph Stuart, Evelyn Thawl, Webb Tilton, William Torpey, Jack Whiting, Jack Wilson, Billie Wirth
Credits: Producer: Max Gordon; Music: Jerome Kern; Lyrics and Book: Oscar Hammerstein II; Musical Arranger/Orchestration: Russell Bennett; Musical Director: Robert Emmett Dolan; Book Directed by Oscar Hammerstein II; Staged by Vincente Minnelli; Choreographed by Albertina Rasch and Harry Losee; Scenic and Costume Designer: Vincente Minnelli. Two acts and 21 scenes. Total performances: 59

"Curtain Time"-a segment of the stage show (Radio City Music Hall, week beginning Thursday, February 22, 1940)
1st number: **"A Sentimental Mood"**
Cast: Loper and Barrat, Earl Lippy, Music Hall Glee Club (Irving Landau, Director)
2nd number: **"Rhumba"**
Cast: Robert Regent, **Loper and Barrat**, Hilda Eckler, Music Hall Rockettes (Dances by Russell Markert; Music by Harl McDonald
Credits: Producer: Russell Markert; Settings: Nat Karson; Costumes: Nat Karson, Marco Montedoro—executed by H. Rogge; Stage Lighting: Eugene Braun

All in Fun (Majestic Theatre, December 27, 1940-December 28, 1940)
Opening Night Cast: Anita Alvarez, Kirk Alyn, William Archibald, **Maxine Barrat** ("How Did It Get So Late So Early?" Dancer; "Love and I" Dancer), Anna Marie Barrie, Candido Botelho, Walter Cassel, Imogene Coca, Christopher Curtis, Fred Deming, Dorothy Dennis, Henry Dick, Orpha Dickey, Hugh Ellsworth, Eleanor Fairchild, Jane Fears, Paul Gerrits, Bob Herring, Peter Holliday, Betty Hull, Bill Johnson, Jane Johnstone, Pert Kelton, Mildred Law, Peggy Littlejohn, Ray Long, Don Loper, Red Marshall, Thersa Mason, Frank Milton, David Morris, Wynn Murray, Marie Nash, Gertrude Nicols, Nancy Noel, Bob Ogelsby, Puk Paarls, Ed Platt, David Preston, Roberta Ramon, Bill Robinson, Miriam Seabold, Dorothy Spelcher, Beverly Whitney, Dorothy Whitney, Jack Whitney, Natalie Wynn
Credits: Producer: Leonard Stillman; Director: John Murray Anderson; Choreographer: Marjery Fielding; Scenic Designer: Edward Gilbert; Stage Director: Edward Mendelsohn; Director (staging): Leonard Stillman; Costume Designer: Irene Sharaff; Music: Baldwin Bergersen and John Rox; Additional Music: Will Irwin and S.K. Russell; Sketches: Virginia Faulkner, Charles Sherman and Everett March; Lyrics: June Sillman and John Rox; Additional Lyrics: Will Irwin, S.K. Russell, Irvin Graham and Virginia Faulkner; Orchestral Arrangements: Charles L. Cook and Hilding Anderson; Vocal Arrangements: Pembroke Davenport; Orchestra Direction: Ray Kavanaugh. Two acts, 25 scenes. Total performances: 3

Biography (Studio M Playhouse, Coral Gables, Florida, March 13, 1958-date uncertain)
Cast (order in which they speak): Michael Nixon (Richard Kurt), Beryl Taylor (Minnie, Marion Froude's maid), Julian Voloshin (Melchior Feydak), **Maxine Barrat** (Marion Froude), John Kelly (Leander Nolan), John Vella (Tiger Wilson), Milton Hahn (Orrin Kinnicott), Jo Herman (Slade Kinnicott, his daughter)
Credits: Producer-Stager: Owen Phillips; Settings and Lighting: Tom McKeehan. Three Acts.

Angel in the Wings (Coconut Grove Playhouse, Coconut Grove, Florida, February 23-March 6, 1960)
Cast: Paul Hartman, Carol Bruce, **Maxine Barrat**, Hank Ladd, Alice Pearce, Tom O'Horgan Lenny Dale, Mildred Hughes, Sandra Donat, Raiston Hill, Chet London

Angel in the Wings (Colonial Inn, St. Petersburg, Florida, opening April 10, 1960-date uncertain)
Cast: intact from Coconut Grove Playhouse production (above)

Filmography

Thousands Cheer (M-G-M, 1943)

Cast: Kathryn Grayson (Kathryn Jones); Gene Kelly (Private Eddie Marsh); Mary Astor (Hyllary Jones); John Boles (Colonel Bill Jones); Ben Blue (Chuck Polansky); Frances Rafferty (Marie Corbino); Frank Jenks (Sergeant Koslack); Frank Sully (Alan); Dick Simmons (Captain Fred Avery); Ben Lessy (Silent Monk); Mickey Rooney (Himself-Emcee at the Show); Judy Garland; Red Skelton; Eleanor Powell; Ann Sothern; Lucille Ball; Virginia O'Brien; Frank Morgan; Lena Horne; Marsha Hunt; Marilyn Maxwell; Donna Reed; Margaret O'Brien; June Allyson; Gloria DeHaven; John Conte; Sara Haden; Don Loper; **Maxine Barrat**; Kay Kyser; Bob Crosby and his orchestra; Benny Carter; M-G-M Dancing Girls; José Iturbi; Bob Crosby; Sig Arno; Harry Babbitt; M.A. Bogue; Georgia Carroll; Wally Cassell; Cyd Charisse; Eileen Coghlan; Charles Cota; Cliff Danielson; Sayre Dearing; Natalie Draper; Dorothy Ford; Jack Gargan; Aileen Haley; Sam Harris; Myron Healey; Betty Jaynes; Willy Kaufman; Robert Keith; Kenner G. Kemp; Linda Landi; Sylvia Liggett; Marta Linden; Barbara Mace; Sully Mason; James Millican; Edmund Mortimer; Odette Myrtil; Bea Nigro; Helen O'Hara; Henry O'Neill; Susan Paley; Peggy Remington; Carl Saxe; Paul Speer; Harry Strang; William Tannen; Don Taylor; Ray Teal; Florence Turner; James Warren; Bryant Washburn; Bunny Waters; Larry Wheat; Eve Whitney; Dick Winslow

Credits: Producer: Joe Pasternak; Director: George Sidney; Writers: Paul Jarrico; Richard Collins; Cinematography: George Folsey; Sound/Sound Designer: Douglas Shearer; Art Director: Cedric Gibbons; Costume Designer: Irene; Composer (Music Score): Herbert Stothart; Musical Direction/Supervision: Herbert Stothart; Set Designer: Edwin B. Willis; Make-up: Jack Dawn; Academy Award Nominations for Best Color Art Direction (Daniel B. Cathcart; Cedric Gibbons; Edwin B. Willis; Jacques Mesereau); Best Color Cinematography (George Folsey); Best Score (Herbert Stothart); Technicolor, 125 minutes

Television Credits

Swing Into Sports—December 22, 1947 (DuMont-owned New York City station WABD, Channel 5)—Joan Kerwin and Chuck Tranim host Maxine Barrat as guest. Also appearing was Latin and American dance proponent and studio owner Don Pallini.

And Everything Nice—November 1, 1948 (Launch of the DuMont Television Network's daytime schedule on that date-January 2, 1950)—Host: Maxine Barrat; Lee Klein; Producer-Director-Writer: Bob Loewi; Assistant Producer: Barnaby Smith; Sponsors: Ameritex Fabrics and A.S. Beck Shoes.

Photographic Horizons—January 12, 1949-March 7, 1949 (DuMont Television Network)—Maxine Barrat frequently models. Joe Costa and Peggy Corday, hosts.

Versatile Varieties—November 11, 1949 (New York City NBC owned and operated WNBT, Channel 4)—Harold Barry hosts Maxine Barrat as guest. Also appearing were the Smoothies, Lee Bristol, Aram Katcher, Jack Lacey, Lola Lee and others.

Once Upon a Tune—March 27, 1951 (DuMont Television Network)—guest star in musical comedy series with regulars Gordon Dilworth, Phil Hanna, Holly Harris and Ed Holmes.

Maxine (third from left) appears on a TV discussion program in Miami.

WITV Channel 17 News—December 1, 1953-1954, exact date uncertain (Ft. Lauderdale, Florida ABC/DuMont affiliate WITV, Channel 17)—Florida TV's first weather girl. Anchorman: Bill Byers.

Weatherwise – Maxine Barrat—December 24, 1954-1956 (Ft. Lauderdale, Florida NBC affiliate WGBS, Channel 23)—Host: Maxine Barrat.

Mystery Disc Jockey—February 13, 1956 (Ft. Lauderdale ABC/DuMont affiliate WITV, Channel 17, and later on Miami NBC affilliate WCKT, Channel 7)—Guest Star: Maxine Barrat emcees variety show, dances; people from studio audience win prizes by unveiling the Mystery Disc Jockey.

Mystery Disc Jockey—February 23, 1956 (Miami, Florida NBC affiliate WCKT, Channel 7)—Guest Star: Maxine Barrat emcees, performs "Who's Got the Pain" from *Damn Yankees.*

To See or Not To See—February 1956-November 1956 (Ft. Lauderdale, Florida ABC/DuMont affiliate WITV, Channel 17)—Host: Maxine Barrat moderates film and stage review panelists Mig Smith, Lillian Claughton, Art Green and Rear Admiral George McCabe; celebrity guests.

Miami Movietime—c. 1956-60 (Miami, Florida NBC affiliate WCKT, Channel 7)—Host: Maxine Barrat

United Cerebral Palsy Telethon—Saturday, January 18, 1958 10:30 p.m.-Sunday, January 19, 1958 2:30 p.m. (Miami, Florida NBC affiliate WCKT, Channel 7)—Emcees: Dennis James, Maxine Barrat, Nancy Reed. Also appearing were Jan August, Gracie Barrie, Cab Calloway, Don Casino, Marion Colby, Don Cornell, Billy Eckstine, Phil Foster, Miss Iris of Romper Room, Irv Kupcinet, B.S. Pully, John Payne, Ritz Brothers, Buffalo Bob Smith and Clarabelle, Step Brothers, the Treniers and others.

About the Author

Kristin Baggelaar, descended on her mother's side from the Ketchams, one of the founding families of the Massachusetts Bay Colony, is related to the Whitman family and the great American poet, Walt Whitman. Born in Glen Cove, Long Island, she has spent most of her life in the greater New York metropolitan area. Among her special preschool memories were listening to Russ Morgan and Sammy Kaye 78 rpm records playing on her grandparent's RCA Victor Victrola console—and whirling around the apartment living room with her grandmother to Patti Page's hit recording of the "Tennessee Waltz." Watching professional dance teams on the *Ed Sullivan Show* made her feel as carefree as she felt while dancing in her grandmother's arms; today *Dancing With the Stars* evokes the same pleasurable feeling, but in her mind's eye it is Loper and Barrat bringing us joy. Her book, *The Copacabana* (Arcadia Publishing, Images of America series), provided a magical gateway into the world of ballroom dancing in its glory years of the 20th century—and paved the way for a friendship with one of its brightest stars, Maxine Barrat.

She is also the author of *Folk Music: More Than a Song*, published by Thomas Y. Crowell, Inc., and by Omnibus Press (London/Sydney) as *The Folk Music Encyclopaedia*.

Index

If you enjoyed this book,
please visit our website
www.midmar.com

or phone or write for
a free catalog

Midnight Marquee
9721 Britinay Lane
Baltimore, MD 21234
USA

410-665-1198

27076316R00150

Made in the USA
Charleston, SC
25 February 2014